DANIEL OST

FLORAL ART
AND THE BEAUTY OF IMPERMANENCE

DANIEL OST

FLORAL ART
AND THE BEAUTY OF IMPERMANENCE

PAUL GEERTS

Φ

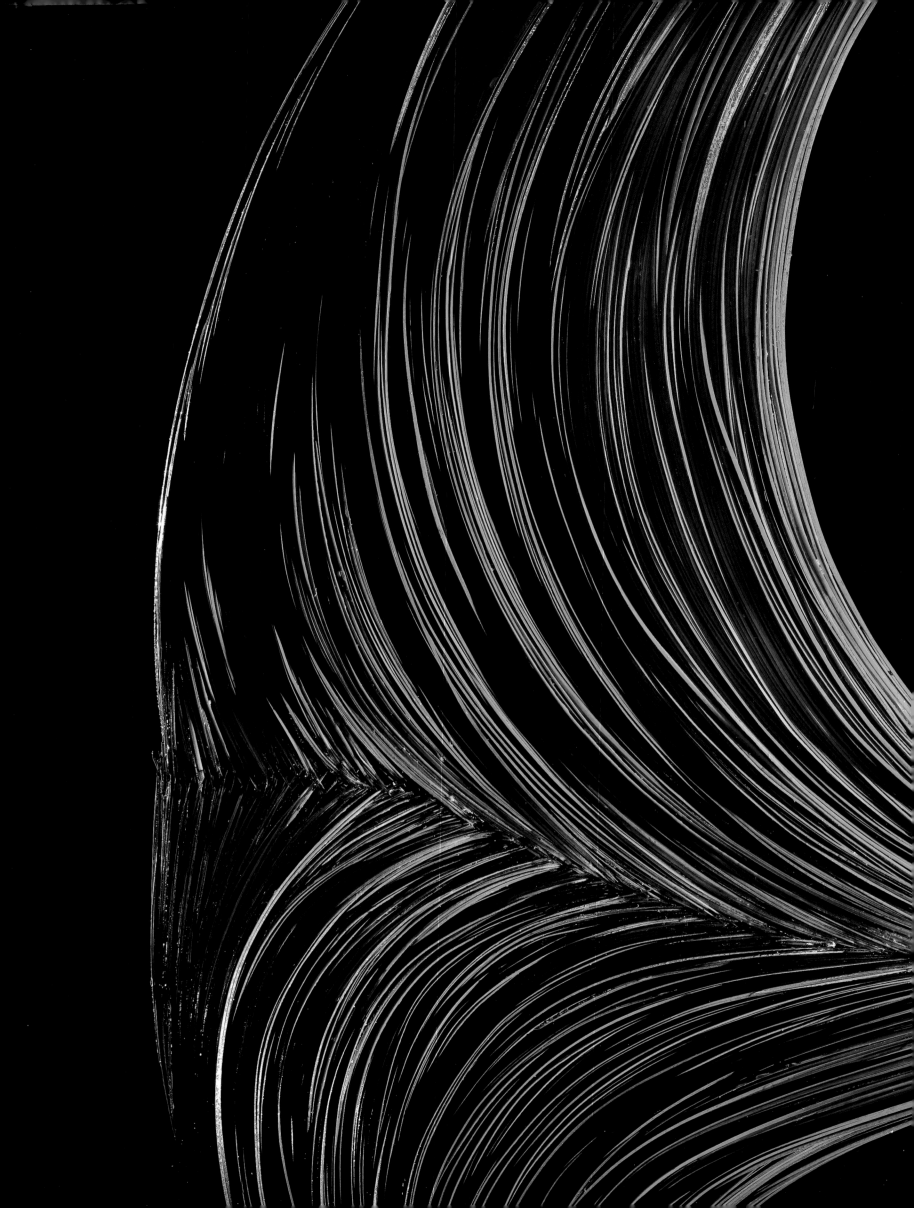

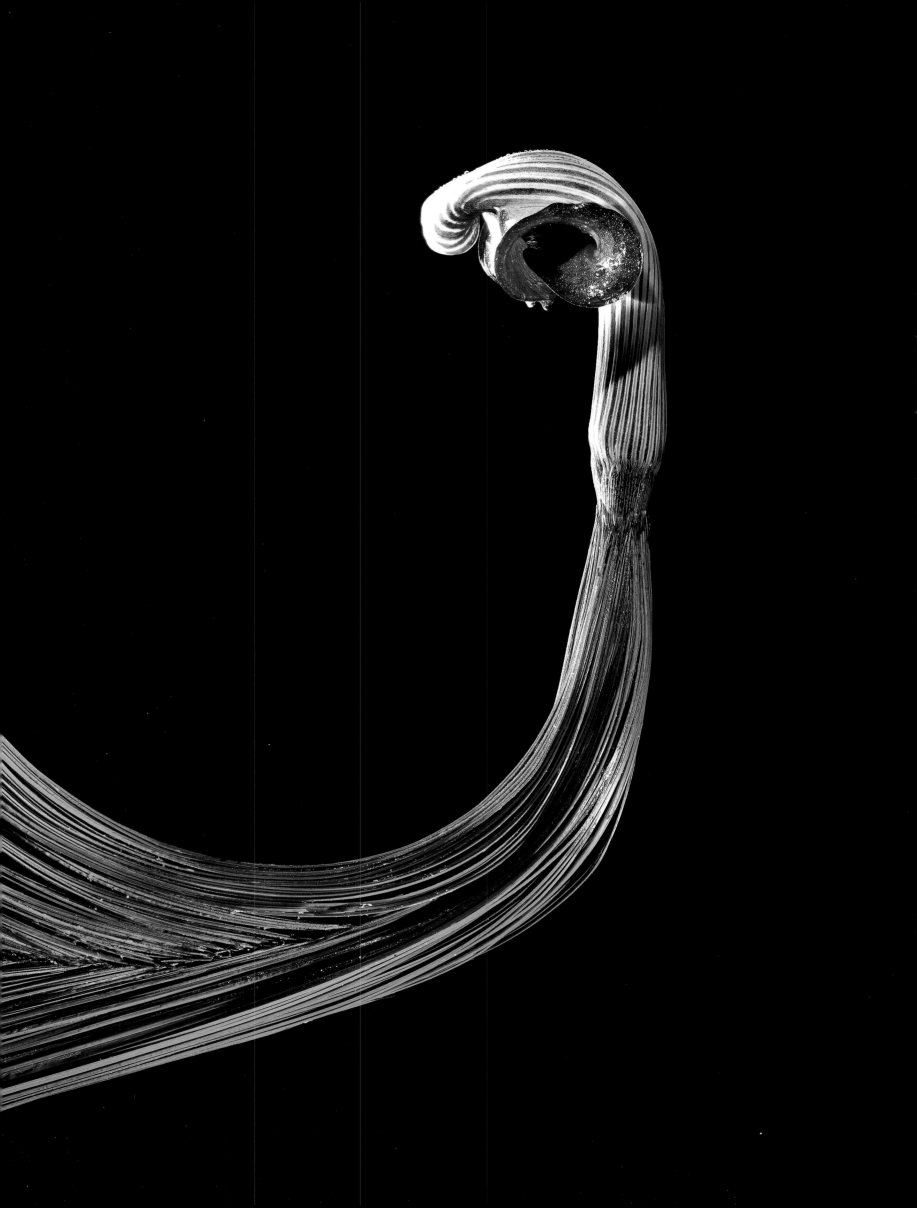

FOREWORD

MARTINE DE CLERCK-VAN DEN WEGHE

I first became acquainted with Daniel Ost's floral and visual language in the early 1980s through his wife, Marie-Anne, who showed me, in their Sint-Niklaas flower shop, the original floral materials used in the classes organized by the Belgian Flower Arrangement Society. On several occasions I had the good fortune to watch magnificent decorations for weddings and other special events take shape in Ost's hands. The idea of documenting these beautiful, transient creations in photographs seemed imperative, in order that the work could be more widely seen and serve as inspiration to others, representing as it did genuine innovation in what was then the very traditional world of flower design. And so the first book was born, *Bladeren in Bloemen I*. It became Ost's calling card and opened up new horizons for him. He developed his art further, in Japan in particular, where he found fresh inspiration to feed his longing for something authentic—something perfect with respect to form, content, and environment.

Compositions of stacked leaves and sculptures made of pruned plants became novel and audacious forms of floral decoration. Ost became a trendsetter. If you asked him why he made such pieces, then the maestro, as I like to call him, would answer, "I begin where others stop." Each creation is a challenge, an occasion for his imagination and creativity to push him to execute new ideas, always more rigorous and ambitious than what came before. Never satisfied, he keeps looking for innovative concepts, stimulated by his surroundings and their history, his knowledge of flowers and plants, his curiosity, and his fascination with forms, materials, and colors in harmony.

The first book was soon followed by a second, and the series grew from there to include such books as *East x West*, which addresses the bridge Ost's work builds between the Zen world of the East and the colorful, abundant world of the West.

Now, in the artist's sixtieth year, we are delighted to present the ultimate anthology of his life's work, *Daniel Ost: Floral Art and the Beauty of Impermanence*. Every piece in this volume is a true work of art, constructed with patience, iron discipline, and respect for deadlines. The maestro himself ensured that every small flower, every berry and stalk, was in precisely the right position. During the preparation of this book, too, he gave his stamp of approval on every aspect of the imagery, the layout, and the texts that evoke the effects of his work and the process behind it.

I am extremely grateful to Ost for sharing his impressive life's work, to everyone who has assisted him over the years, and to all those whose ingenuity and energy have contributed to the realization of this volume. I invite you to enjoy every page and to cherish the exquisite natural beauty.

This was all once a dream. Now it is the jewel in the crown!

A single *Vanda* orchid is accompanied by a protruding "hand" of charred wood that reflects the shape and colors of the vase.

PREFACE

DANIEL OST

If life is but a passage,
At least let's sow flowers on it.
     –Michel de Montaigne

This book tells the story of my life as a flower designer. It is the fruit of my restless quest to find new ways of adding an extra dimension to the beauty of flowers and plants—beyond how they flourish in their natural environment. A quest, too, for the balance between the technical perfection of flower arrangement and the imperfect human heart.

Flower design is a creative challenge. It is an attempt to express, using a beauty that already exists, even more beauty, by means that are virtually unlimited in regards to form, color, and other considerations. The beauty of plants is an ongoing challenge, an ongoing demand for attention. You have to see them, feel them, smell them. You have to try to understand them before you can work with them.

It is precisely for this reason that flowers demand total mastery and discipline. They are living things that do not always do what their handlers hope they will, despite sound expertise. In addition, we have to reckon with time as a constant opponent. Flower design illustrates the temporal, the ephemeral, like few other disciplines. Flower designers have to convert fresh vegetal materials into new forms in a short period of time. During this transformational process we try to let nature express our intentions and to convert the coincidences and technical obstacles into something useful. Each step of the process must be mastered by the maker's strong will and mind, including the critical choice of each vessel, which must be in perfect harmony with the material, an ultimate symbiosis between vase and plant. The vases take on the role of the soil, the natural support of flowers and plants. In addition, an intense relationship develops with the space in which the creations appear. There the work exists while, at the same time, the composition itself changes the space.

I have lived at odds with the world, and even with myself, but never with my flowers. Flowers are my medium. They represent what lives within me and what I find impossible to express by other means. They convey my moods, my feelings. Working with them helps me in the search for the why of things, the essence of my being. With my flowers I feel like a very small part of a much vaster whole. Giving ourselves up entirely to the things we love, the joy of creation, fills us with a feeling of freedom and fulfillment.

This book also bears witness to my other passion: the Far East, in particular Japan. When I first visited Japan more than thirty years ago, it was love at first sight—love for the people, for

It is thanks to this photograph of two roses in a vase covered in thorns that Daniel Ost was invited to Osaka for the 1990 world championship of flower decoration.

the plants, for the nature and the culture. Since then my love has only grown wider and deeper. Of course I am and remain a Westerner, a child of Brueghel. But my encounter with Japan influenced me profoundly, as a flower designer and as a person.

Each culture has a different approach to flowers and what they have to tell us. I grew up in a culture in which the art of flower arrangement held a utilitarian and decorative function. It served to embellish buildings and played a symbolic role in life's important events, such as a birth, a wedding, or a death. In such cases it is especially the form and color of a flower that we let speak. In the East I discovered a culture in which flowers and leaves are used to convey thoughts, in a manner that relates to the soul of the flower. As the Japanese poet Ueshima Onitsura writes:

Silent flowers

speak also

to that obedient ear within.

In flower arrangement in Japan, contemplation is more significant than observation: things in nature can be the subjective reflections of one's own mind. Not only the outward appearance of a flower, but also nature and feeling matter, especially in this regard. It is about the aspiration to really belong to nature in its entirety.

In contrast to Western culture, which the human-centered perspective takes precedence over nature and all other life-forms are subordinate to human activity, the traditional cultures of the Far East place humans in a position of humility. We find ourselves in the middle of, and in harmony with, nature, neither dominating nor controlling it. Eastern art demonstrates a refined courtesy with regard to natural, defenseless things. It cherishes the beauty that we only perceive if we have sufficient patience and watch very closely, with a love for what is imperfect, natural, and essential. This, in Western society, is sometimes difficult to find.

Flowers and plants have associative meanings, for instance, the cherry blossoms that mark the end of winter and represent the continuity of life, or the lotus, whose pure and brilliant flowers emerge out of the mud, recalling Buddha's pure doctrine growing out of an imperfect world. Capsule, flower, leaf, and bud can be combined in a single arrangement so as to symbolize past, present, and future.

I wish to convey my thanks to all those who contributed to this book. First, my loyal team in Belgium, who have assisted me everywhere and in all circumstances with endless patience and solved the most difficult problems, at impossible moments, thanks to their distinctive craftsmanship. Thanks also to my many collaborators and students in Japan, Russia, and other countries, on whom I can always call to help carry out my wildest dreams.

Deep thanks to my daughter, Nele, my hope in days of fear, who, together with her husband, Yann, keeps the business ship afloat and my future in safe hands. No other flower matches the beauty of this one, who I've watched burgeon and bloom.

Lastly, I wish to pay tribute to Marie-Anne, my faithful rock, without whom none of this would have been possible. Words, even flowers, are not sufficient to express my gratitude.

A tightly structured bouquet made in the 1990s, featuring the subdued earthen colors of *Iris germanica* 'Beige Butterfly' and cat's-tail in a rare bronze vase, is proof that, from the start, Ost was in search of the perfect harmony between flower and container.

NATURAL MYSTERY

CEES NOOTEBOOM

The difficulty begins with the name. What do you call what Daniel Ost creates? A flower arrangement? Certainly not. And still, you have the feeling that if you leave out the word "flower," you leave out something essential. But what *do* you call it? Sculpture? Sculpture doesn't breathe the way this does. A work of art? That goes without saying; it's art, and it's very clearly work. The ancient Greeks point us to the answer, as they so often do. Their word *technè* embraces all the meanings pertaining to these creations: craftsmanship, clever handiwork, art, system, method, and technique, but also—as Homer uses it—cunning. "In a negative sense," my Greek dictionary adds, but I don't believe it. Can I call Ost cunning? When we spoke I didn't ask him, and maybe it's just as well, though I could have explained that Homer always calls Odysseus cunning, and that I consider Odysseus one of the most inspiring figures in world literature. Maybe because of that very cunning, which gets him out of one predicament after another and often saves his life.

But what does this have to do with the Belgian Ost? What is so cunning about this man? Is there a link between cunning and art? I think so. All art, if it is good, outwits death. A seventeenth-century flower painting by that other Flemish artist, and other Daniel, Seghers, still sparkles with the same color and clarity as it did the day it was painted. But that work was made

This controlled composition of green cornus with Italian berries was created for the Tō-ji, one of the oldest and most important Shinto shrines in Japan.

with oils, which can endure for centuries. Ost, on the other hand, works with the most perishable of materials: flowers, grasses, twigs, leaves, reeds, fruits, vegetables. Ephemeral, cut off from the source of their sap and so condemned to death, shrouded in the curious, final beauty of that moment. Ost outwits death by colluding with it, by giving what was doomed to perish a whole new life in art. He takes a form that nature creates and repeats with only the most minute variations—a birch twig, an azalea, a tulip, a tuft of reed, a ginkgo, a rose, an autumn leaf—and makes something that has never been made before. What emerges, whether through the transformation of a single plant or through a masterful combination of diverse elements, can never be re-created by another artist in the same form. If it were, it would be plagiarism, just as surely as if a painting or a poem had been stolen.

But if these works are so perishable, how can I know so much about them? I know because Ost is doubly cunning. He knows that his creations will perish sooner or later. But if a master photographer records them, they will last forever. So Ost has found his kindred spirit in the photographer Robert Dewilde, and so I am looking at the mysterious sculpture of an *Aspidistra*. I realize I've used the word "sculpture" in spite of myself, but there's no way around it. After all, how *do* you describe this fiercely green, exquisitely lit construction of sharp *Aspidistra* leaves reaching upward and running downward, coming together as they snake past one another, a construction closed at the bottom, then fanning modestly open, only to close once again and continue upward as it began below, with the cool, vertical simplicity of stems?

When Lucio Fontana slits or perforates the flat surface of a monochrome painting, he creates a unique work of art that could only be a Fontana. The same is true of Ost. There's no point in describing his compositions in words. Zen simplicity and restraint, conveying the essence of a single plant, alternate with Flemish-Burgundian excess, all this nourished by his almost religious respect for his materials. One moment his work is whimsical; the next you gasp at his unflinching quest for basic contradictions. A leaf folded into a cube, hundreds of bamboo shoots—it seems anything is possible. Ost can transform nature without doing violence to it.

And the longer you look, the easier it is to forget that each work is a victory in a struggle against time, that the creator of all this diversity must forever be aware that the materials he holds are perishing imperceptibly. And how diverse this diversity is! One composition suggests a Japanese temple; the next a Constructivist painting or an art nouveau lamp. This man's hands can create anything his mind can conceive.

To get to the bottom of these riddles, there are a hundred questions I would like to ask Ost, but he's expected in Japan and I'm in Spain, so we talk on the telephone. I've seen him in a photograph—a still-youthful man who could have stepped out of one of Hermann Hesse's novels. His soft Flemish accent is charming in a way the harsher Dutch of the north rarely is. He tells me that there were military men in his family and that he once attended a military academy. The discipline he learned there certainly serves him well in his chosen profession.

At the age of twenty, Ost went to work at a florist's. Fortunately for him, the Dutchman Peter Curfs had found his way to Ost's hometown of Sint-Niklaas, not far from Antwerp. Curfs had once run a celebrated flower shop, Sheherazade, in the Hague. Ost says he learned a tremendous amount from Curfs. Soon he was on his way to Holland, the land of flowers, to learn more. And it

Archetypal figures of red cornus, which
surface in Ost's work in a range of variations,
here sit on typical Flemish cobblestones.

wasn't much longer before he had won his first prizes: he placed second in the European flower-arranging championship in 1983, and in 1985, earned second prize in the world championship in Detroit. Suddenly he was the center of attention in Hong Kong, Taiwan, and Japan. Since then Asia, and especially Japan, has become part of Ost's life; he has flown there 170 times in recent years.

The two of us talk about the madness that takes hold of Japan every year when the irises bloom, and I tell him about the hundreds of Japanese people I have seen painting with watercolors in Kyoto's botanical gardens or sometimes practically crawling *into* the flowers, tripod and all, for a photograph. We discuss ikebana and ikenobō, how the Japanese art of flower arrangement has petrified under centuries of domination by the same families, how it must conform to inviolable and immutable laws dictating the ceaseless return of stylized and identical forms. How great is the contrast with his own art, which never repeats itself. Not that this does any harm to his legendary status in Japan—quite the opposite, in fact. Then he tells me that in Asia he gets homesick for Flanders. I say that I would like to stop by his shop-studio on my way back from Spain to the Netherlands. He hesitates and says I won't see anything there like the photographs of his work.

When I arrive, I see that this is true and yet not true. Ost's wife, Marie-Anne, runs the shop, which in no way resembles an ordinary florist's. It is located on a square in a small provincial town, but once you step inside, the door shuts on the everyday world. Everything around you seems rare and precious; you wander through a realm of enchantment that slowly takes hold and grows ever stronger.

A Japanese woman is braiding birch twigs into an intricate form; outside, small autumn leaves fleck the shimmering green duckweed on the pond with crimson; a moss-covered whale-bone fans outward. I ask and repeat the names of flowers I have never seen before. And when, an hour later, I find myself back outside, I am holding a tan autumn bouquet for my mother, surely the most beautiful arrangement anyone has ever made for her. Of course, it is true that it cannot compare with the unique creations of Ost, but it is also true that in an enchanted place, inspiration can blaze to new heights—heights where plants and flowers in the hands of an artist undergo a metamorphosis unlike any witnessed before.

Ash-treated clay slabs in the Tō-ji represent the many ancient writings that are housed in the temple. The swirling spiral in the background, incorporating four hundred thousand berries, symbolizes the road to the hereafter.

THE ART OF INTEGRATION

KENGO KUMA

Daniel Ost stands on his own, venturing through his work to challenging places where no one has gone before. These new territories are unclassifiable—neither flower arrangements nor gardens, neither sculpture nor architecture. And yet, oddly enough, when I see the work, something feels incredibly familiar. It brings to mind the nests that are produced by creatures in the wild. Those nests are constructed according to very exacting standards—standards that dictate the collection of twigs and pebbles to create a shelter, for the animals themselves and for raising their young. There is no reason to think that these animals ever considered such an abstract notion as beauty. Nevertheless, their nests are astoundingly beautiful. And like nests, Ost's creations are simple yet complex and beautiful, all at the same time.

At some point, human beings divided the concept of nests into various categories. From nests emerged the fields of flower arrangement, landscape gardening, sculpture, architecture. Humans appreciate vertical structure; they like to create hierarchies by ordering things into categories and, within those various areas, imposing rules and aesthetics that only they can understand. Over the course of time, these vertical hierarchies proliferated, until the similarities they once shared with nests were completely forgotten. This is a sad reality of civilization.

This three-dimensional "painting" of fading eucalyptus leaves was created in a freezing-cold chamber to keep the coloration under control.

It seems to me that Ost is attempting to return to the archetype of the nest. He appears to be trying to bring all of these divisions back to their original form. Japan plays an important role in this process. Throughout Japanese history, these categories have been integrated within the scope of gardens. For example, architecture is a part of the garden, rather than something separate from it; there was no such specialized career as that of an architect. Or consider Sen no Rikyū, known as the originator of the Japanese tea ceremony, who sought to integrate everything about drinking tea–that is to say, everything that surrounded him during the primitive act of taking the plant into the body. Tea, flower arrangement, art, garden, architecture. All of these things are incorporated into the *sadō*, or "tea ceremony." In Japan this tradition of integration has existed for centuries.

Ost is more aware of Japan's inherent potential than many native Japanese. He understands how modern society might be salvaged from the standstill that has resulted from compartmentalization. That may be why his creations blend so uncannily with traditional Japanese architecture. I have repeatedly witnessed the way that his works have revitalized ancient buildings.

I often find inspiration from Ost's creations. Why, I'm ready to abandon my own career as an architect in the pursuit of a new integrated field that transcends categorization. But this path is by no means easy. In our complicated world, where things associated with nature have suffered to such an extent, it is far from straightforward to return to the nest. I have been stunned to see just how weary Ost is after completing one of his designs: a shadow of himself, like an exhausted mother bird after she has built a nest and raised her young. It made me realize the sheer effort and concentration that Ost's nest-like creations require, and the difficulties involved in executing these projects in modern times. It arouses a whole new sense of admiration for his accomplishments.

Right: A sculpture of steel grass stands in the Tō-ji.

Following page: A choreography on the beach of Zuydcoote in northern France: an anthropomorphic figure of lead-armored tree bark with strings as blood vessels and a wavy crest of staghorn fern is intended to evoke a Greek warrior on the beach of Troy.

METAMORPHOSES

A BEAUTY PREVIOUSLY UNKNOWN

Daniel Ost has always pushed boundaries. He has never limited his palette to flowers, but called upon all sorts of unexpected materials found in nature, such as leaves, trunks, branches, rinds, thorns, roots, seeds, cones, fruits and vegetables, mushrooms, moss, and grass. This is now standard for many flower designers, but when Ost started out, it was unprecedented and controversial. He remembers vividly his winning piece in the first Belgian championship he entered, in 1979: a composition of tree trunks, branches, and leaves, which, for lack of money, he had gathered in a park in the Ardennes.

Ost frequently uses ordinary materials from his immediate surroundings—recycled or found things that, like the objets trouvés of the Dadaists and surrealists, undergo a genuine metamorphosis in his competent hands. The following pages feature several of his early "metamorphoses." These three-dimensional vegetable sculptures include budding lotuses on a little bed of blocks of red cabbage; a cube of blossoming leek stalks under a railway bridge; a column of autumn leaves from the city park; a hammock of red cabbage leaves filled with squashes and suspended on bamboo poles on the beach; a burned-out window frame with duckweed and hydrangea flowers on a pond; a circle of poppy leaves on a puddle of water. The inventive use of unexpected materials is a constant.

Some of these pieces bring to mind the work of celebrated land artists such as Andy Goldsworthy, David Nash, and Richard Long, all of whom Ost deeply admires for their ability to transform an existing environment, sometimes with minimal interventions, using materials that are available on site, in a way that redefines the relation between humans and nature. But there are also substantial differences between land art and Ost's projects. In Ost's work, one always feels the hand of the technically driven florist, and his creations are infinitely more detailed, executed with a far greater degree of finish and craftsmanship.

Flower arrangers everywhere can credit Ost with having expanded their palettes with flowers and plants that were previously unavailable in the regular trade. Simple garden flowers such as hydrangeas, snowdrops, violets, and sweet peas, and wildflowers such as white water lilies, poppies, butterbur flowers, and even dandelions have captured his imagination. So have the rare plants in the collection of Belgium's Arboretum Kalmthout and botanical garden—both feasts for the floral gourmand. He loves as well special varieties of common and less common ornamental plants, preferably in exceptional shapes and colors. His many encounters with Japan have offered another rich source of vegetable wealth, further feeding his floral creativity. To name a flower or plant that he has not yet handled would be difficult indeed.

Ost pushes boundaries not only in his materials, but also in the way in which he uses them—almost literally controlling them, processing them into autonomous, freestanding creations, practically new life-forms in themselves. In his words:

> Working with leaves or flowers need not result in a copy or a reproduction of nature.
> That is mere deception and will result in failure. You cannot improve on nature.
> If you realize that, and you still assert the right to remove flowers and plants from
> nature, but then don't succeed in doing something at least equivalent, you are bet-
> ter off letting everything grow where it is. My wish is to make something with these

The banality of both the material (leek flowers) and the location (a railway bridge in Sint-Niklaas, Belgium) is easily forgotten thanks to the harmony of form and color.

vegetable materials that did not exist before, a beauty previously unknown. In this the material has to be seen as a substance; only then is it ready to be transformed into a new form. At the moment I cut a flower, it ceases to be a flower. It becomes a material, like the painter's pigment or the sculptor's stone, which I shape through my mind.

Ost follows many paths in doing this: the endless repetition or stacking of leaves and flowers, the deconstruction and reconstruction of vegetable material, vegetal mimesis, unusual combinations. This book abounds with brilliant examples of such metamorphoses with "a beauty previously unknown." New types of roses composed of rose petals; "paintings" of discolored eucalyptus leaves or common butterbur, blue or red berries, ginkgo leaves, cherry blossoms, chrysanthemums, or orchids; mille-feuilles of red cabbage leaves; fans and sunshades of pine needles and horsetail; stained-glass windows of autumn leaves; vegetal choreographies and still lifes made of callas, poppies, narcissi, peonies, buttercups, and lotuses; woven and wrapped lotus and aspidistra leaves, cornus branches, willow and spindle, bamboo, and steel grass.

These compositions often allude to geometric shapes—spheres, circles, cubes, cones—or to archetypal forms with a symbolic or mythical significance, such as peaks, pillars, arcs, spirals, cupolas, or pyramids. But also the sun and the moon, or a star-filled sky. Or anthropomorphic figures: a warrior in armor, a group of Buddhist monks, a statue of Saint Francis, a dancing couple. One can see in this an attempt to seek the essence of a sculpture and the very meaning of nature itself.

If Ost deals with his vegetable materials in a stunningly creative manner, he is also an enormously talented craftsman who has mastered the most difficult techniques from both Western and Eastern floral decorative traditions. It is one thing to have ingenious ideas, but quite another to be able to realize them with a material that is frequently stubborn and highly perishable. In his

A young Ost works with his wife, Marie-Anne, in 1987 at an unusual spot: the landfill in his hometown of Sint-Niklaas.

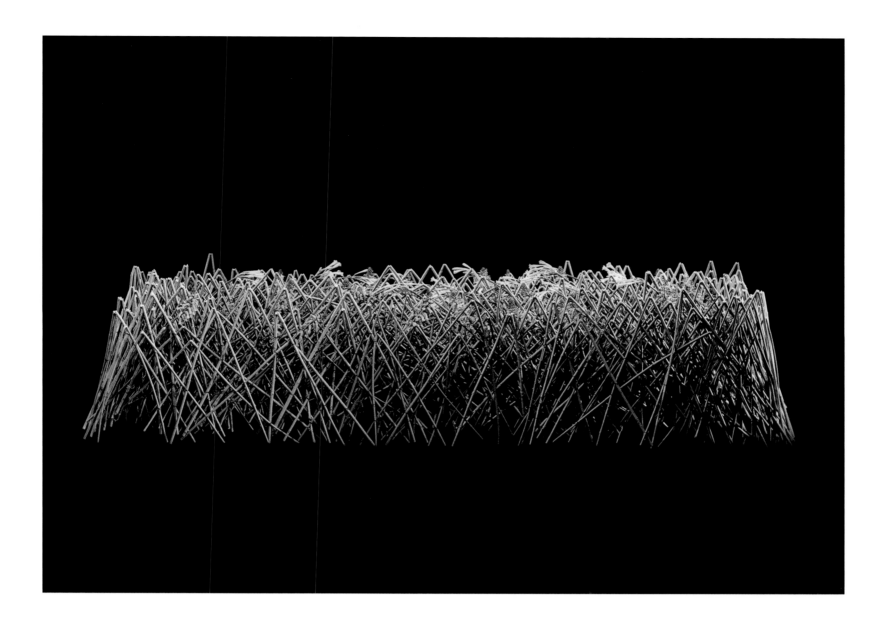

search for a new floral aesthetic and a perfect symbiosis between vase and flower, he was one of the first designers to weave and wrap flower stalks. In the late 1980s he was the first to use glass test tubes to provide water to the flowers in his sculptures—a method he picked up from a sixteenth-century herbal book by the Italian botanist Giovanni Battista Ferrari that is now used by almost every flower arranger. "We cannot throw traditions and craftsmanship overboard, but neither can we let them take the upper hand," Ost says. "We must use them to support creativity so that flower arrangement becomes a contemporary means of expression, fueled by the soul of its maker."

An intriguing spring creation for the Tō-ji in Kyoto combines young branches of *Cornus sanguinea* 'Viridissima' with flowers of the tiger lily, *Lilium bulbiferum*.

Left: A vegetal interpretation of Maurice Ravel's *Boléro* at the landfill of Sint-Niklaas features swelling clay hills and dancing leek flowers.

Above: A sphere of pine bark rests in the sand at the Sint-Niklaas landfill.

Following pages: A cardboard wave movement with seed cases of honesty, *Lunaria annua*, enlivens the sand at De Ster, a recreation area in Sint-Niklaas.

Time, place, weather, and seasons are integral
parts of Ost's work. Here, a monumental
wickerwork of weeping willow and cornus
appears in the Drowned Land of Saeftinghe,
the flood area along the river Scheldt
on the border between Belgium and
the Netherlands.

On the Belgian coast, a hammock of red
cabbage leaves filled with butternut squashes
hangs on giant bamboo sticks.

Ost is always creatively influenced by the surrounding environment. Here, the buds and leaves of the lotus—one of Ost's favorite flowers—in small cubes of red cabbage seem to float on Belgium's river Scheldt.

A ceramic bridge created by the artist Lebuin D'Haese along the river Zenne in Belgium is decorated with fruits of *Dischidia pectinoides*.

Above: Wind catches a grass sculpture in the Drowned Land of Saeftinghe, Belgium.

Right: In an old orchard in the Belgian town of Weert, this installation evokes the Biblical tree of knowledge, or perhaps a cornucopia with the mouth of a reed snake and apples rolling out.

Following pages: Waves of iris leaves wash ashore where the Japanese iris, *Iris ensata*, blossoms. This is a reference to Kūkai, the founder of the Shingon school of Buddhism, who came ashore at the Tō-ji upon his return from China.

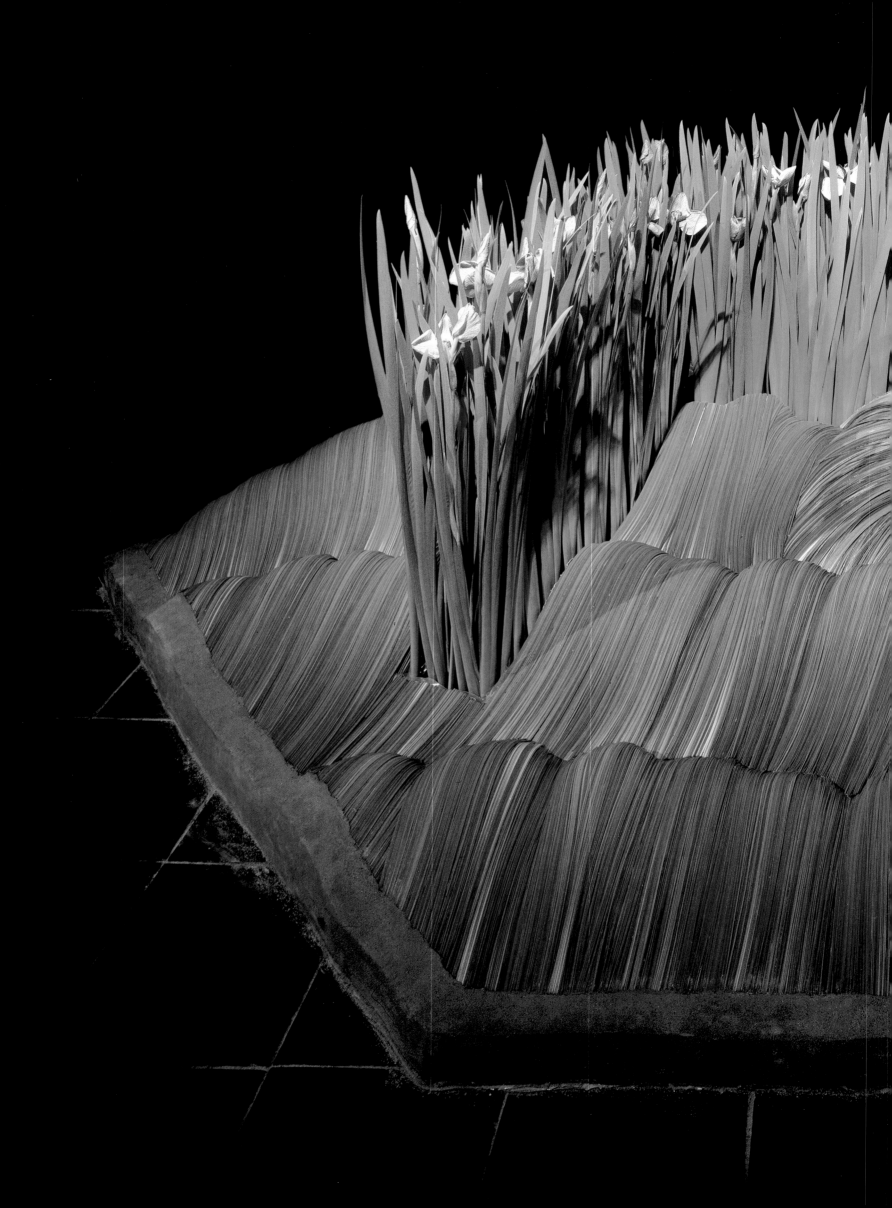

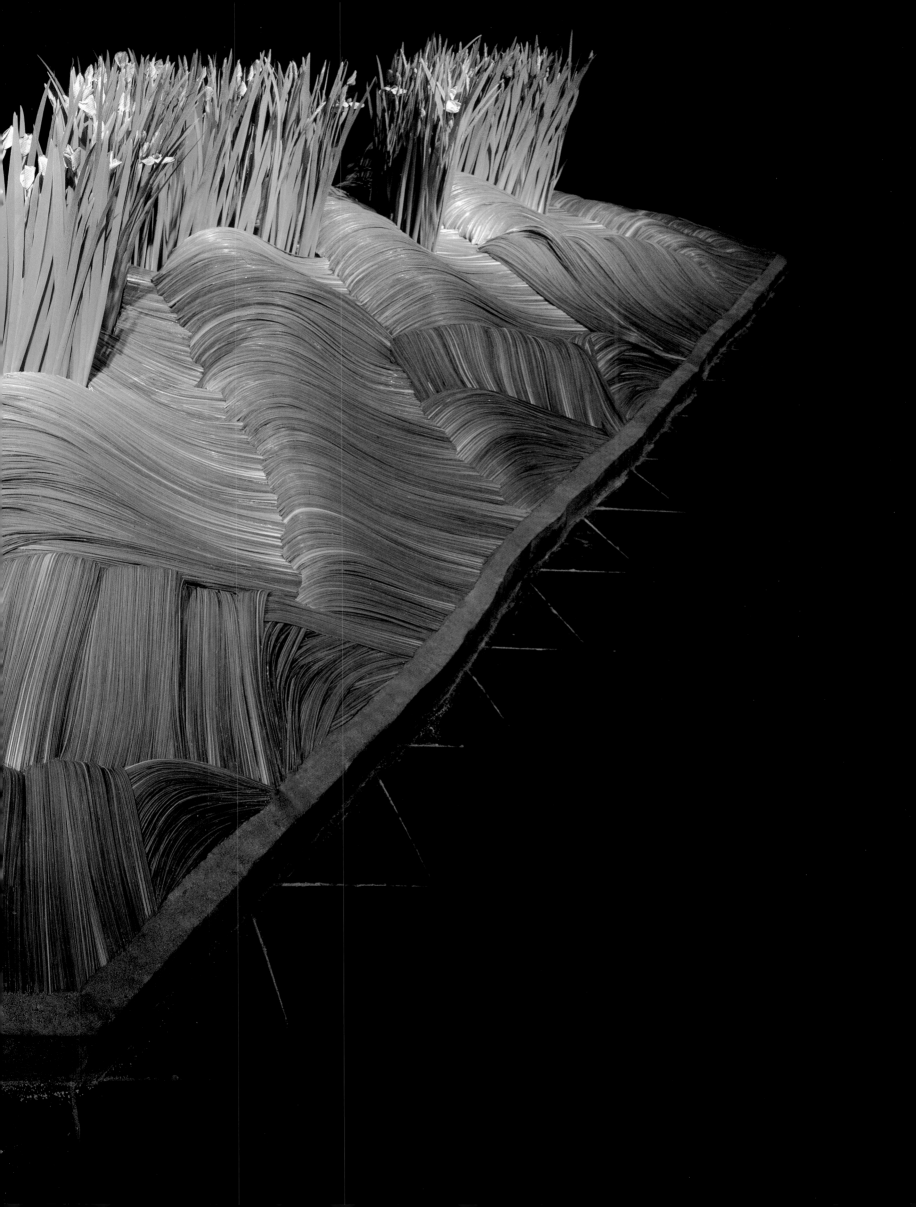

Duckweed, delicate hortensia flowers, and
snowball berries drift on the water in a raft
of charred wood.

Like a painter uses pigment and a sculptor
uses stone, a flower designer uses leaves,
flowers, and berries as a palette. Ost's
composition calls upon the blue berries
of *Prunus spinosa* and hortensia leaves.

Ost experiments with forms and materials, line and volume, curvature and geometry, to discover a new floral aesthetic. At left, woven structures of *Encephalartos laurentianus* and *Larix decidua* were installed on the landfill of Sint-Niklaas. Above, a composition with eucalyptus and *Elaeagnus x ebbingei* leaves was glued, one tiny piece at a time, onto a form in Ost's garden.

Drawing in the sand at the landfill of Sint-
Niklaas, the artist explores his floral palette
with the buds of the South African coffee
bush, *Brunia albiflora*.

Cornus branches and coral
take on architectural form.

In the process of deconstruction and reconstruction, new forms emerge from combinations of vegetal material. At left, a structure built with the leaves of *Strelitzia reginae* and the dark flowers of the Persian lily stands in a field in the Waasland region of Belgium. Above, chunks of oak wood and clematis tendrils form a ball at the landfill of Sint-Niklaas.

A whalebone frames a ball of cypress
needles at the landfill of Sint-Niklaas.

Art on the landfill offers a visual, three-dimensional sort of poetry: a dance of dandelions and rocks made of conifer needles.

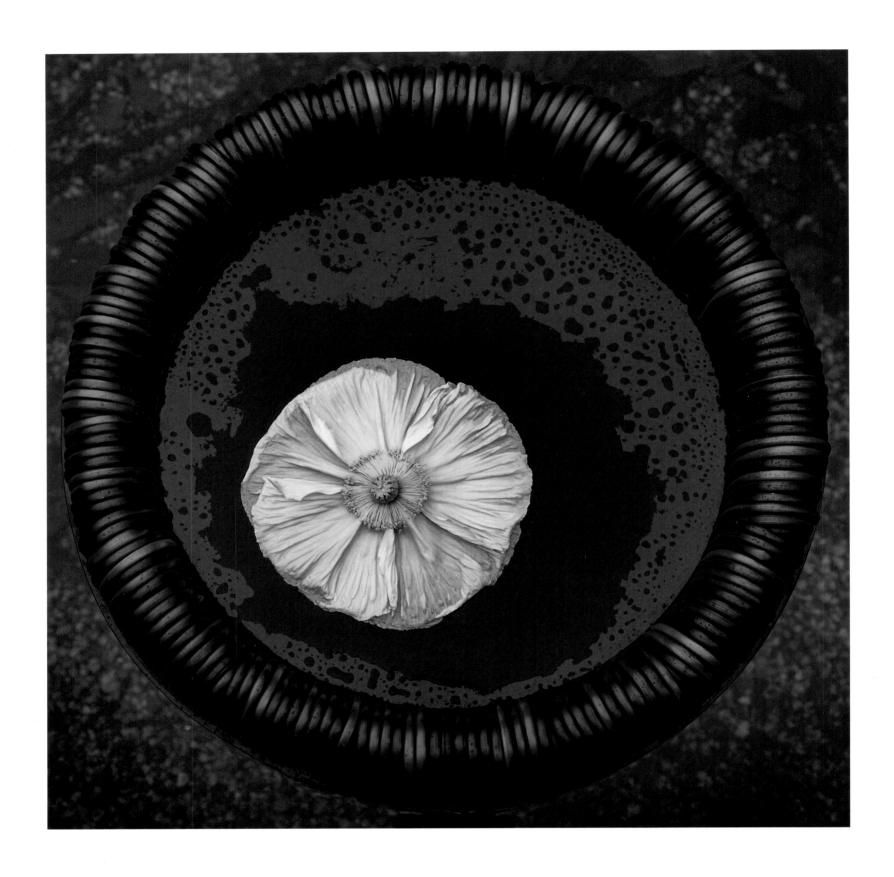

Separated from their life source and therefore
destined to disappear, cut flowers take on the
mysterious beauty of their own approaching
end. Here, a single poppy flower adorns a
crown of *Scirpus* on a glass pane.

Sensual transparency was apparent in Ost's
work long before he first visited Japan.
Above, a nest of ice measuring sixteen
inches rests in a market fountain in the
city of Lille in northern France, with leaves
of baby's tears delicately placed atop.

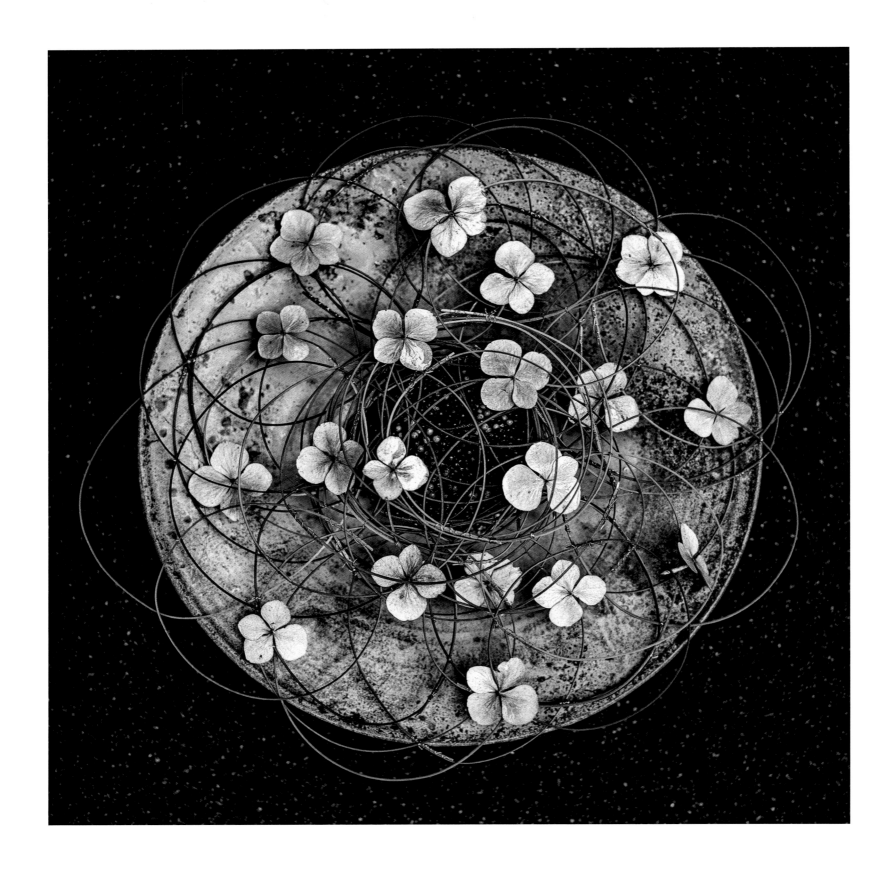

A floral still life from Ost's workshop in
Sint-Niklaas has elderberries and graceful
hortensia flowers floating on a lacework
of bear grass.

White calyxes and yellow cores of narcissi
evoke the image of the sun and reference
Narcissus himself gazing at the flowers in
the water.

Left: When the petals of the Florence rose were tucked in this porcelain vase by the ceramicist Roos Van de Velde, the vase itself, as well as the petals, transformed into a flower.

Above: These sixteen-foot-long lily stalks were set on the bottom of the Oude Schelde river, then woven, bound, and photographed the next morning as they bloomed.

Flowers, and especially poppies,
represent transience and fragility.

Form, color, and texture: a board built
out of the gray leaf of the common
butterbur is adorned with the red flowers
of *Celosia cristata*.

Gray edelweiss and these narrow vases
crafted out of the dried leaf of the common
butterbur create a unique relationship
between flower and container.

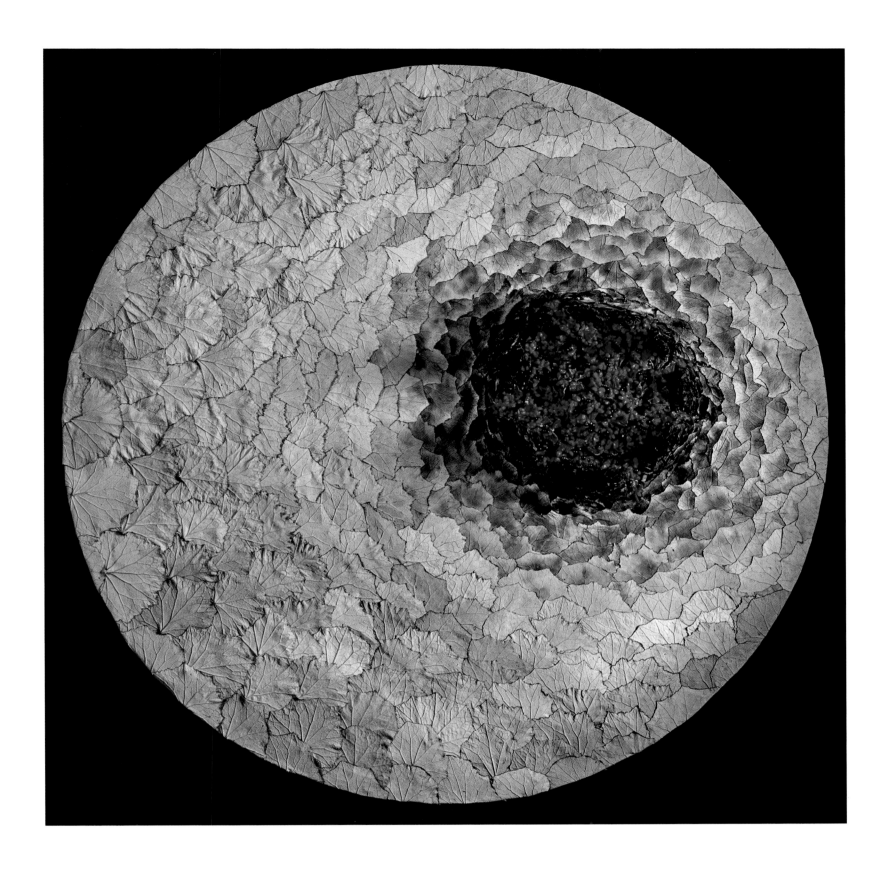

Maximum effect with minimum means:
"banal" vegetal materials, such as the leaf
of the coltsfoot, are transformed into a
new life-form.

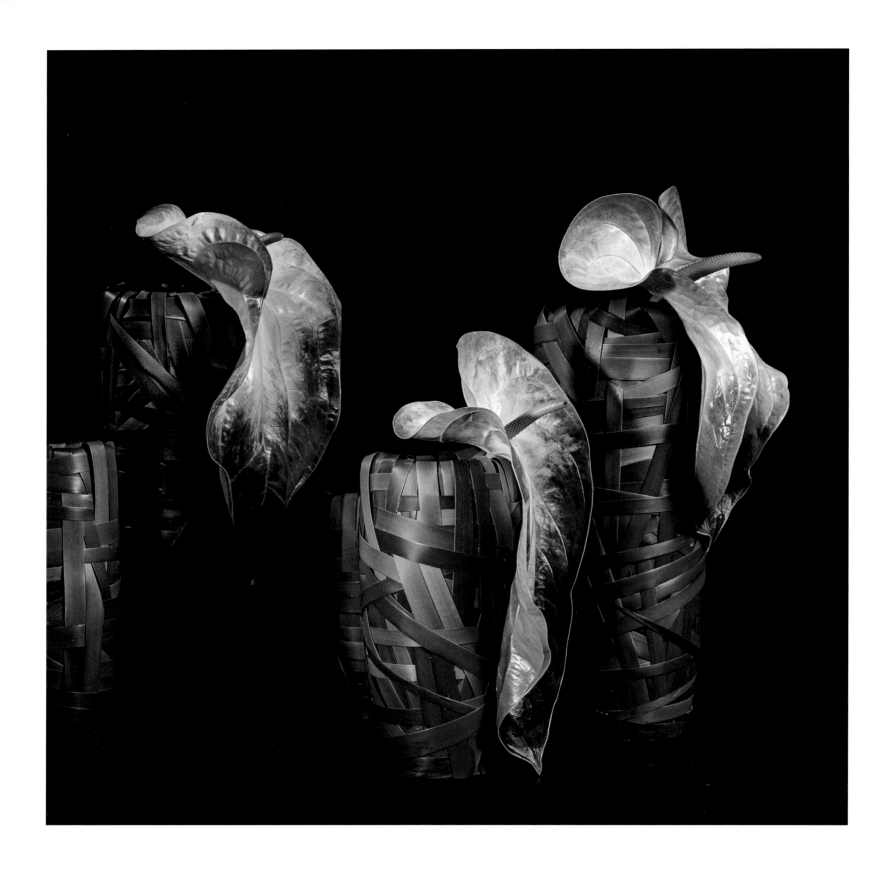

Two examples of harmony in form and color between flower and container: above, a sculpture nearly a yard high of marbled *Anthurium* flowers in vases of woven cats'-tails; at right, flower stalks of the Japanese Jack-in-the-pulpit, *Arisaema sikokianum,* with tendrils and fruits of the passion flower in an oxidized metal vase designed by Emiko Nakamura.

Above: A modest ode to the Flanders
Fields poppy suggests that despite
the many young lives sacrificed there,
life shall always bloom anew.

Right: A mille-feuille of stacked autumn
leaves refers to endless repetition, creating
a new reality in which the original materials
are saved from oblivion.

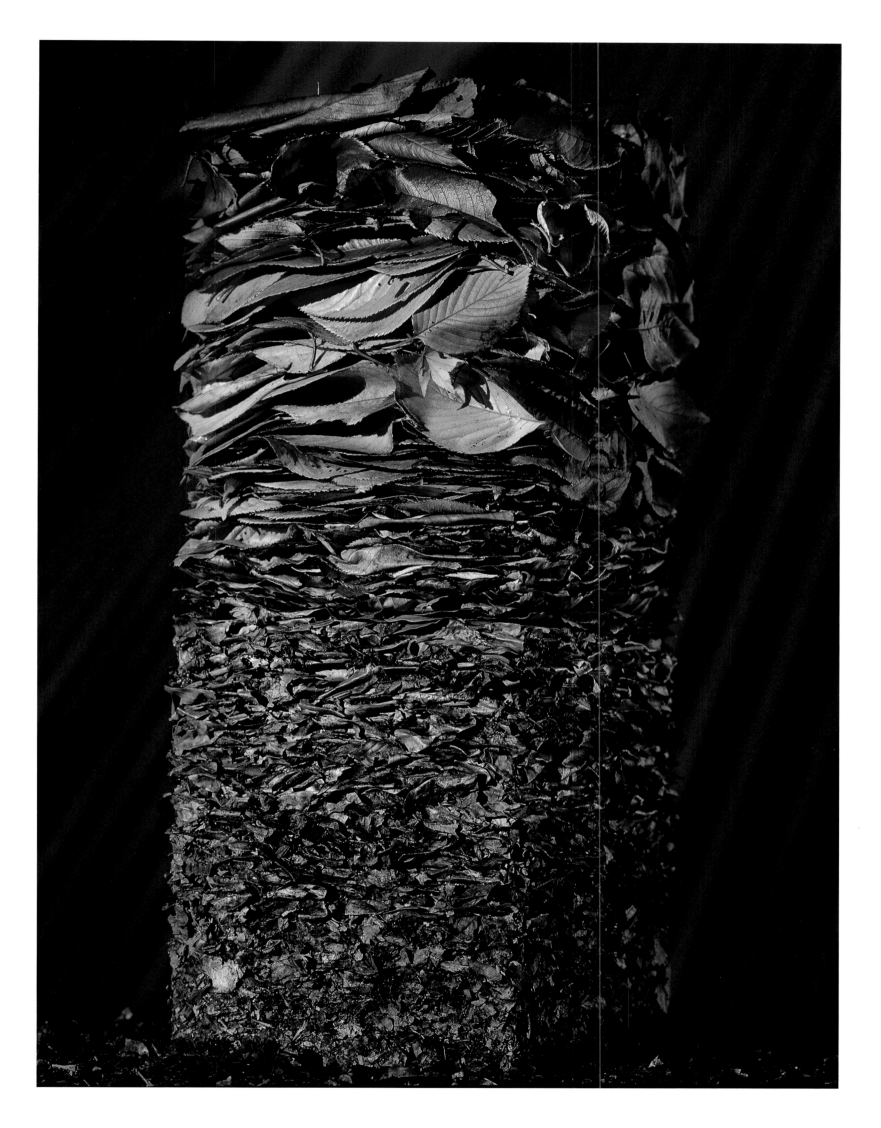

This Burgundian tableau uses pumpkins
from the garden of Ost's close friend,
the late EU commissioner Karel Van Miert.

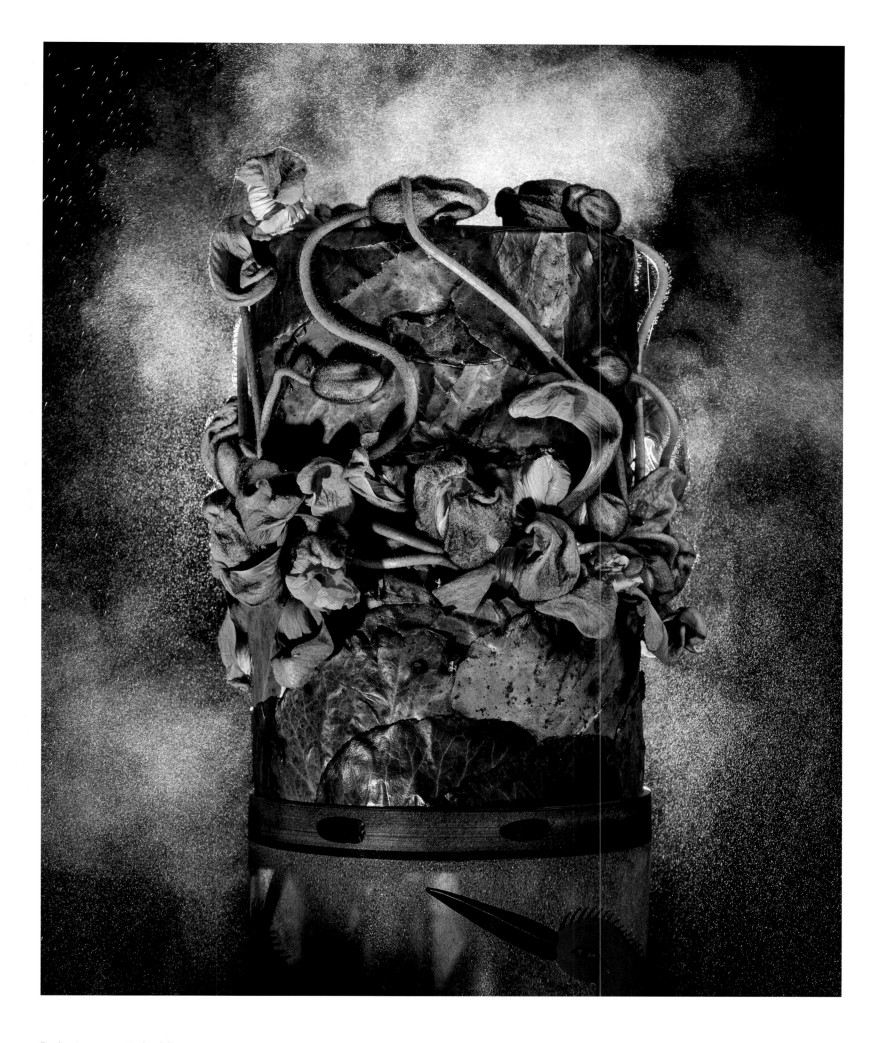

Decline is apparent in the delicate
flush of the poppy and half-decayed
Bergenia cordifolia.

Only when we accept the material as
substance, and not as a miniature version
of nature, is it ready to take on its new form.
Here, an existing rose is transformed into
a new shape with additional rose leaves.

A unique, massive Tantansai silver shell holds
rose petals as if they were mother-of-pearl.

Art nouveau remembered: sensual bouquets feature uncommon flowers and unusual fruit in elegant vases. Above left, a composition with tree peonies and *Enkianthus* in an antique bronze vase from the Han dynasty; above right, a bouquet of brown *Eustoma* in a unique glass and wrought-iron vase by the Czech architect and designer Bořek Šípek; and below, a bouquet constructed around a range of colored capsules from rare magnolias in the Botanic Garden Meise, Belgium.

A flamboyant autumn bouquet with subdued colors in harmony with the vase calls to mind Jan "Velvet" Brueghel. This piece features dozens of distinctive flowers, plants, and fruits from the garden of the late Jelena de Belder of the Kalmthout Arboretum, a treasure trove for a young flower designer in search of new materials.

A bouquet measuring more than a yard high, made for an exhibition in 2010 at the Seibu Ikebukuro Gallery in Tokyo, consists of about thirty different flowers and plants, among them a new and extremely rare Asian buttercup that is not yet available on the market.

A coiling sculpture of red cornus decorated with False Freesias *Anomatheca laxa* in the Tō-ji represents the spiral of life.

Above: A structure in the form of a tagine is made of corn husks and the berries of the so-called bee bee tree or *Tetradium daniellii* var. *hupehensis*.

Right: The essential forms and exquisite materials of this organic still life, set on a table crafted from a six-hundred-year-old elm tree, are reminiscent of the Japanese tea ceremony.

Floral geometry: this abstract artwork with
green bananas and Murano glass by Venini
was created for an exhibition in Hong Kong.

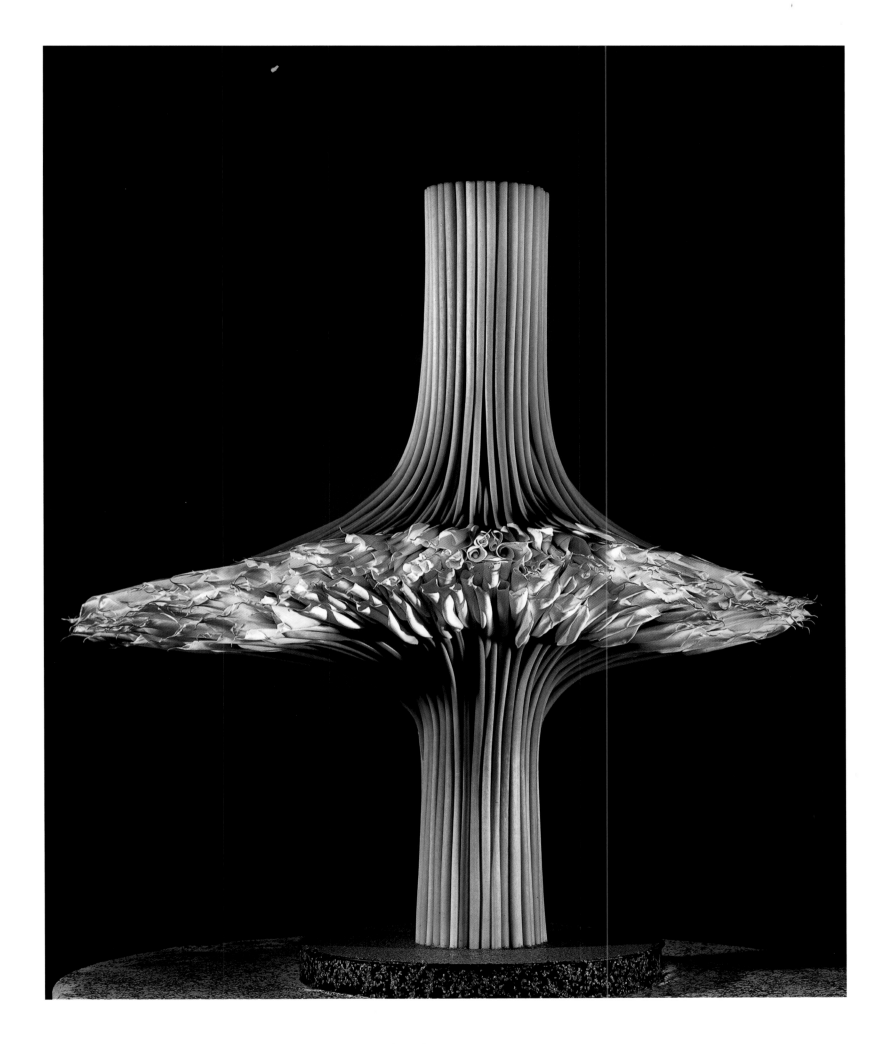

Ost transforms natural materials into ever-new forms and figures with ingenuity and craftsmanship. Sometimes such precision requires trial and error: he had to start over more than ten times to achieve this structure with white arums, because the piece kept falling apart.

Above: Stacked magnolia leaves echo a singular vase by the Japanese master ceramicist Ken Matsuzaki for an exhibition in Tokyo.

Right: An eccentric flower rises like a phoenix from a mountain of charred bamboo. This orchid–a unique specimen of a new, prize-winning, extremely expensive cultivar– was cut by the Japanese cultivator as a gift to Ost.

Left: *Muscari* flowers complement a silver vase by the Belgian artist David Huycke.

Above: Ost designed this pyramid of berries as a tribute to his Japanese master, Noboru Kurisaki.

Simplicity is not a characteristic of the
beginner, but the hard-earned hallmark
of the expert as exemplified by these sober
compositions using longleaf pine. At left, a halo
with a narcissus as the bright sun; and above,
an overturned branch with several little roses.

Above: A subtle composition in the Sugimoto Residence in Kyoto focuses full attention on the spectacular crimson *Disa uniflora* orchid from South Africa.

Right: Flower decoration at the intersection of various disciplines in the Tō-ji: the red *Disa* orchids glow like fire on the black weaving of charred bamboo.

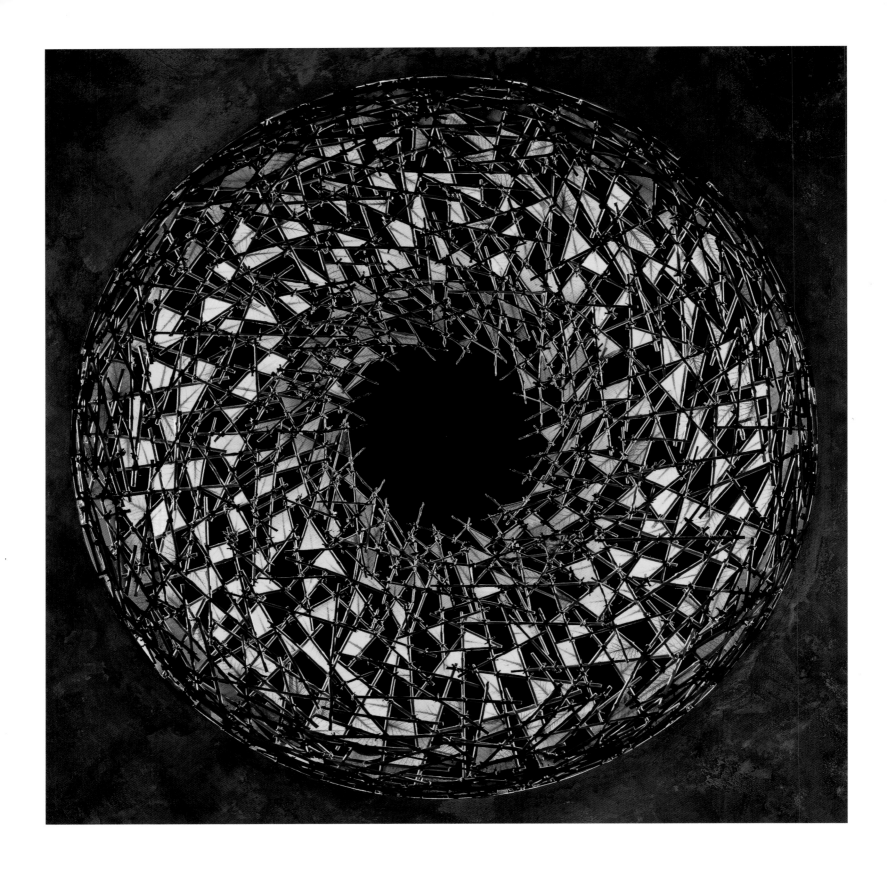

Above, right, and preceding pages: Glowing,
melancholy colors of autumn are captured in
Gothic "stained-glass" windows made of fallen
leaves—symbolizing the coming of winter and
the eventual return of spring.

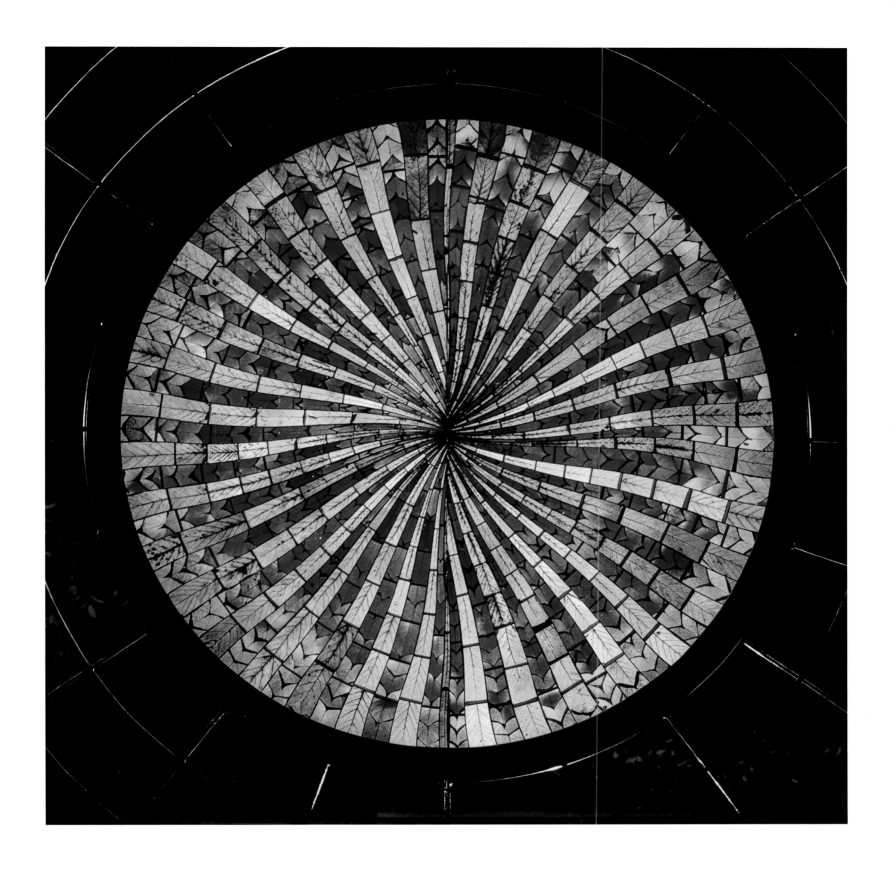

EXHIBITIONS

IN SEARCH OF
THE GENIUS LOCI

Daniel Ost has participated in numerous exhibitions over the years. They sometimes take place in the most exclusive and extraordinary locations, for example, the Buddhist temples of Ninna-ji, Tō-ji, and Kinkaku-ji in Kyoto, or Izumo-taisha in Izumo, where he was the very first Westerner invited. He has shown his work in the Roosenberg Abbey in Waasmunster, Belgium; at the highly esteemed Sogetsu School of ikebana in Tokyo; the historical Sugimoto Residence in Kyoto; the Ōhara Residence in Kurashiki; and in prestigious hotels and retail stores.

Ost understandably devotes a great deal of attention and enthusiasm to exhibitions. Free of any specific commission or commercial pressures, and with the help of a flock of faithful collaborators, he can carry out his floral passions to the fullest. He also has at his disposal the most exclusive flowers, plants, and other materials. This often leads to astounding and compelling creations. Some are executions of ideas that have been germinating in his mind for years, while others emerge in the moment, inspired by a specific setting, an encounter with a special vase, the availability of a particular flower. The location and the season are always integral as well. He prefers to use flowers and plants that are typical of both the season and the region.

Ost strives to create an intense relationship with the space in which he works, even as the presence of his work necessarily transforms that space. He might carry out a formal reflection on the architecture, choosing the layout or the colors to call out particular characteristics of the environment, its specific atmosphere, its particular visual patterns. Or the relationship may be more a spiritual one, in which the works grasp the ambient character in an abstract, symbolic, or metaphorical manner, for instance through plants that refer to the history of the place or to its cultural

Left: Architectural bamboo sculptures line the entrance to Kinkaku-ji, the Temple of the Golden Pavilion, in Kyoto. The door frames a lavish spring bouquet.

Above: Pillars of candle wax more than a yard tall are capped with red berries of *Ilex verticillata*.

Preceding spread: This modest ode to the imperial chrysanthemum, a symbol of the life-giving sun, perfection, longevity, and happiness, was designed for the ceremonial space of Ninna-ji.

or religious significance. Examples include his compositions with imperial chrysanthemums in Ninna-ji, the Chrysanthemum Temple, and his work with lotuses, the holy plant out of which the Buddha was born, which represents cleanliness, purity, inner growth, and connectedness with the universe. By incorporating archetypal forms or visual metaphors, the works engage in a symbolic, allegorical dialogue with both their surroundings and their spectators.

Ost hopes that viewers will not simply behold the beauty of the flowers or the purely decorative value of his compositions—he also wishes to stimulate their minds, to invite them, through his tableaux, to look at the environment in a more conscious manner. It becomes a particularly spiritual journey of discovery when, for instance, the setting is a historical building, a Buddhist temple, or a Catholic monastery. Examples include his sculptures in Japanese temples that are meant to represent a plume of incense, or that symbolize the moon or the sun; spiral-shaped structures that represent humankind's turbulent path through life, the journey to the gods, or progression toward enlightenment; bamboo shapes that reference Kōbō Daishi, the founder of Shingon Buddhism; or a fiery halo around the statue of Saint Francis in the abbey of Waasmunster.

The works created for exhibitions are often spectacular for their vast dimensions, the large quantities of flowers and plants used, and the exceptional quality or extreme rarity of their materials. But they may also be quite intimate, like precious miniatures or minimalist masterpieces, perhaps composed of just one or a few flowers.

The exhibitions frequently draw thousands of visitors, who observe Ost's masterful compositions made out of thousands of berries or pine needles, leaves massaged into shapes, woven grass and branches, stacked pumpkins, whirling petals, or flowers that are just budding or showing themselves in their full glory. As they admire the fragile beauty of the work, they inevitably wonder how it is even possible. How does Ost imagine these creations, and then realize them? How it is possible to shape or weave the branches in this way? To stack or suspend those berries and leaves? To present those flowers so perfectly? It demands great craftsmanship and years of experience, but also a rare audacity and an almost pathological drive for perfection. "That is a constant in my work, that drive for finish and perfection. The perfection almost has to radiate from it," Ost says. "Time is unimportant in this regard. I sometimes work for days on a single piece before it is really finished." For him, the difference between the ordinary and the extraordinary lies in the details. "The more difficult something is, the quicker it perishes, the more I like to work with it. Take poppies, for instance. I may use a couple of thousand, such that the first ones have begun to wilt when the last ones are inserted. I need that tension. It can't be too simple." In this regard, he is very demanding, both of himself and of his associates:

> Sometimes, in the middle of a project, I see that I can do something even better. And then I care little about money or people, including myself, and that is the way it will be and must be. My greatest drive is the fact that I am rarely really satisfied. With each project I question myself anew, regardless of the consequences. That gives me the strength to always continue and want to renew myself. But it also creates unrest. During the design process and the entire preparation of a piece, I live in a state of intoxication, a mental unrest that ensures that I remain critical and always dare to adapt. Until, that is, the moment when something is ready: then I immediately let go.

A truckload of lavender was required to create this stream at an exhibition in the Belgian city of Temse dedicated to the city of Provence. An allusion to Vincent van Gogh's sunflowers is in the background.

SUGIMOTO RESIDENCE
KYOTO

Sugimoto is the largest traditional town house, or *machiya,* preserved in Kyoto, and it is still the property of the Sugimoto family, who made their fortune trading textiles. The family built the residence in 1743 during the Meiji period. After a fire in 1870, the building was entirely reconstructed according to the original plans. The succession of rooms are separated by wooden walls and paper sliding doors, making the layout easily adaptable. Ost exhibited here for the first time in fall 1997, and again in spring 2002. He found his inspiration in the building's history and architecture, and in the seasons as well.

Cherry blossoms welcome spring into the house. The colors and forms of the walls and windows dictated the colors and forms of the installations. Left, a snaking sculpture of clay, covered with the ash of cherry trees and decorated with the leaves of *Ternstroemia gymnanthera,* leads toward a structure made of cherry tree branches and blossoms; and above, cherry blossoms and duckweed float in a geometrical pond.

Following pages: A room-size sculpture of clay, moss, and Chinese poppy seeds takes the form of a Japanese mountain landscape.

A grass sculpture stands in the Buddha
room, reminiscent of incense rising.

Humankind's endless movement is captured
in a spiral of woven cornus branches.

A precious shrine is adorned with vegetal
still lifes reduced to essential forms.

Ost converts natural materials, with great respect for their growth patterns and rhythms, into archetypal forms with strong symbolic or mythical meanings: a pyramid, a spiral, a sea urchin.

KENROKU-EN
KANAZAWA

In 2000 Ost exhibited in the famous gardens of Kenroku-en, in the center of Kanazawa, Japan. Kenroku-en is open to the public and is one of the three great gardens of Japan. It was created between the 1620s and the 1840s by the *daimyō* (warlords of the samurai caste) of the feudal Maeda clan, one of the richest in Japan during the Edo period. Unlike many classical Japanese gardens, which are designed to be viewed from a specific vantage point—for instance, a tea house or a temple—Kenroku-en has several viewpoints that are meant to be discovered sequentially while walking through the site. Kenroku-en literally means "the garden with the six characteristics" that define the perfect landscape: spaciousness, privacy, artifice, antiquity, water, and scenic panoramas.

Above: A sculpture of woven Japanese spindle branches serves as a bed for the Japanese calabash.

NINNA-JI
KYOTO

Ninna-ji is one of the oldest and most important temple complexes of Kyoto. It was erected in 888 by the emperor Uda and is today the main temple of the Omuro school of Shingon Buddhism. Until the nineteenth century, a member of the imperial family was always the chief priest of the temple, and today it still sustains a close bond with the imperial family. Emperor Hirohito hid from the Americans in this temple at the end of World War II. Ninna-ji is also known for its beautiful gardens, which have served as the model for many Japanese temple gardens, and is the seat of the renowned Omuro School of Flower Arrangement. For his exhibition in fall 2004—the first time in history that a Westerner exhibited there—Ost made extensive use of chrysanthemums, or *Kiku-no-hana*, the imperial flower par excellence and symbol of Ninna-ji, which is also known as the Chrysanthemum Temple.

Left: For this "painting" with berries of *Smilax china*, Ost drew his inspiration from Mark Rothko—an artist Ost admires for his ability to render the essence of his medium through color and form.

Above: An archetypal design contrasts the red berries of *Smilax china* with a background of driftwood.

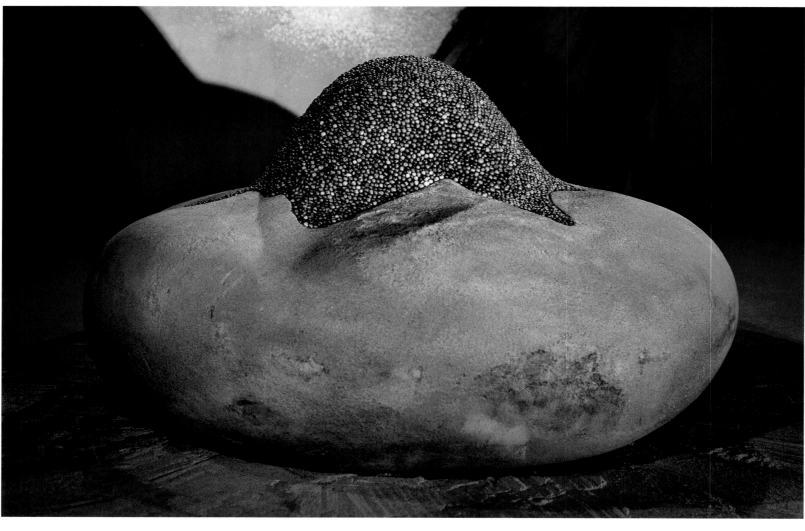

Above left: An architectural installation made of moss-covered apricot branches and Japanese magnolias on a carpet of moss creates a dialogue with the building.

Below left: A clay design treated with the ash of cherry trees and multicolored porcelain berries, *Ampelopsis brevipedunculata,* makes it seem as if the ground is breaking open.

Above: Rare chrysanthemums on a stave harmonize with a screen of *washi* paper by the renowned Japanese artist Eriko Horiki.

Above: A swirling tribute to the imperial chrysanthemum occupies the *Shiro-shoin*, or reception hall, of Ninna-ji.

Above right: White chrysanthemums on dried cherry petals and clay shards carpet the *Kuro-shoin*, the "black" reception hall of the temple complex.

Below right: A structure of steel grass ornamented with the flowers of gypsophila 'Million Stars' recalls a snowy mountaintop.

GANA ART GALLERY
SEOUL

Seoul's Gana Art Gallery is South Korea's most important gallery for modern and contemporary art. Established in 1983, it has grown into a multicultural institution that offers opportunities to both prominent and promising Korean artists, promoting them worldwide. In addition, the gallery regularly organizes high-profile exhibitions featuring such established and emerging Western artists as Pierre Alechinsky, Antoni Tàpies, Sam Francis, Jasper Johns, Roy Lichtenstein, Joan Miró, Karel Appel, Georg Baselitz, Tom Wesselmann, Jean Dubuffet, Georges Braque, Andreas Gursky, Thomas Ruff, Rodney Graham, and Thomas Struth, among others. In his major solo show at the gallery in 2004, Ost created strong relationships between the often monumental vegetal sculptures and the timeless work of the renowned French architect Jean-Michel Wilmotte.

Left: An elegant sculpture of red cornus rests in the open-air theater of the Gana Art Gallery.

Above: This "cactus" landscape is actually made out of needles from the Japanese black pine, *Pinus thunbergii*.

Vegetal surrealism: woven willow branches
and scattered potatoes exemplify how
Ost fashions pure beauty out of the most
commonplace materials.

Vegetal arte povera: paper bags are recycled as
delicate containers for equally delicate poppies.

Three almost-monochromatic grass sculptures engage in a subtle dialogue with vase and surroundings. Above left, love grass with butcher's-broom and horsetail; below left, a room-size grass sculpture—almost sixty-five feet long—made of *Equisetum hyemale* and *Petasites japonicus*; and above, lovegrass with the black flowers of *Cosmos atrosanguineus* 'Black Beauty' in a handmade vase made of *Carex conica*.

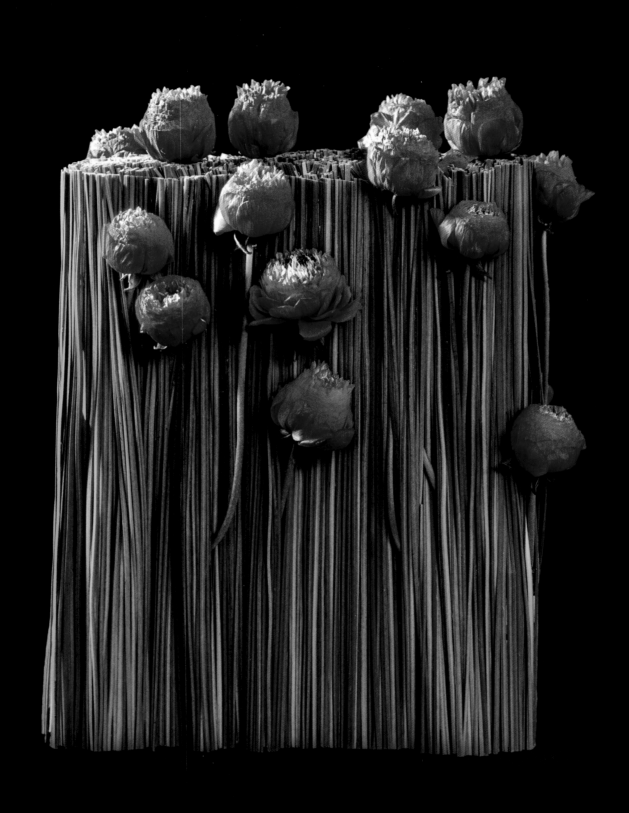

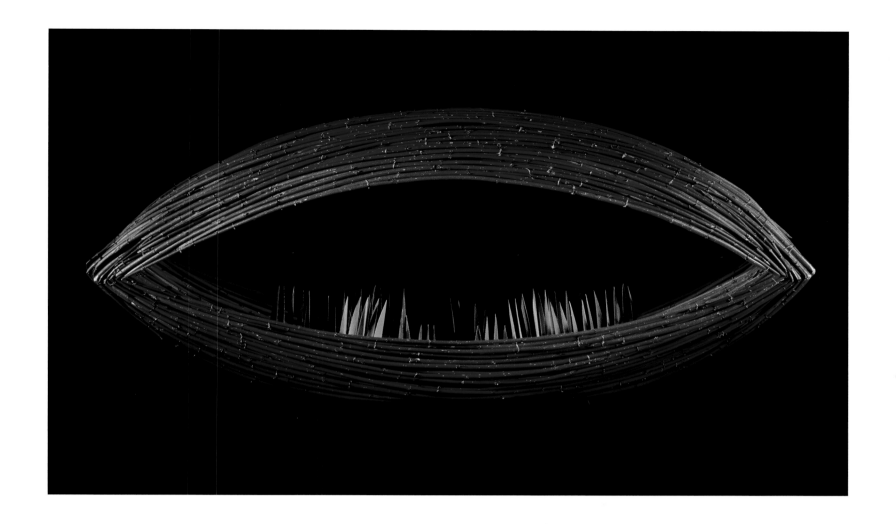

TOUR & TAXIS

BRUSSELS

At the Daniel Ost Experience Days in 2005, 2006, and 2007, the Belgian public became acquainted with Ost's floral creations, which until then had mostly been exhibited in Japan. These events took place in the distinctive setting of the Royal Warehouse on the site of Tour & Taxis in the heart of the Belgian capital. The name, Tour & Taxis, comes from the German aristocratic house of Thurn and Taxis. This family founded postal services in Europe and until the eighteenth century organized postal distribution from Brussels. In the late nineteenth century, the Belgian railway company built an enormous complex on the site for the clearance and storage of goods. The activity in the complex peaked in the 1960s, but lost its purpose with the creation of the European Customs Union. In recent years, it has enjoyed a process of urban renewal. The impressive Royal Warehouse, designed by the architect Ernest Van Humbeeck, is a fine example of functional industrial architecture. Under the glass roof, the main Inner Street and the galleries and offices lining it are bathed in soft daylight. The successful renovation of the Royal Warehouse, the storerooms, and the Hôtel de la Poste was completed with great respect for their history and heritage.

Two stylized faces of spring: at left, exuberant
Persian buttercup blossoms, *Ranunculus
asiaticus*; and above, the delicate green of irises
that are just peeking out from the ground.

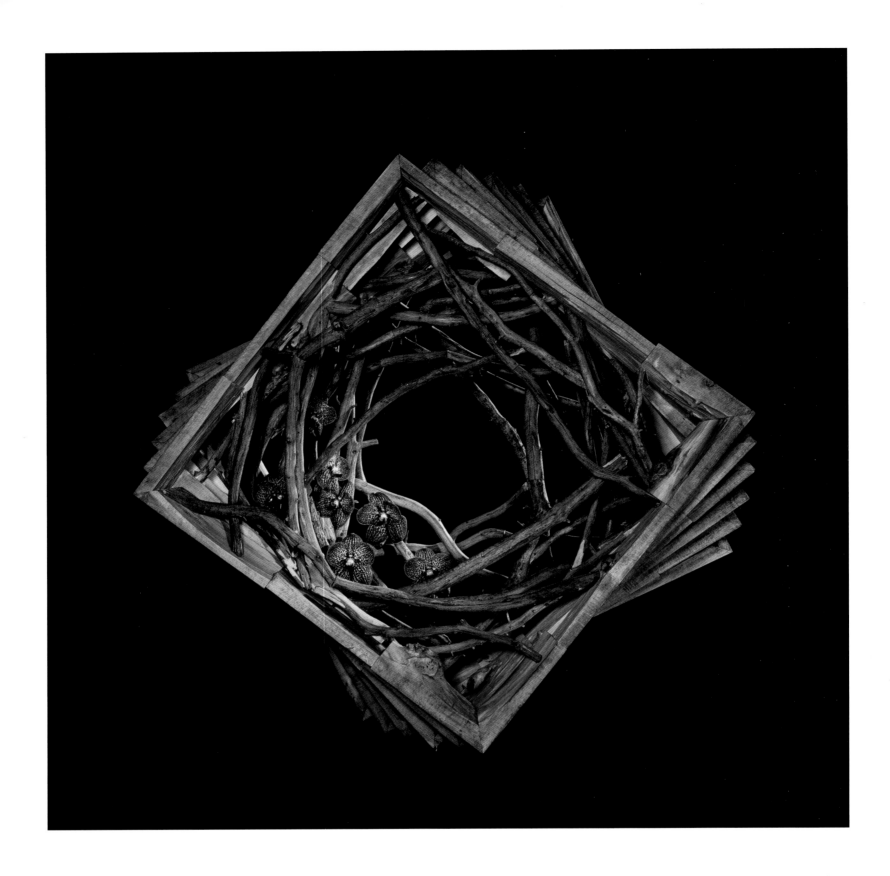

Minimalist flower arrangement geometries:
left, driftwood and *Vanda* orchids, and
right, green and red cornus represent
the transition from summer to autumn.

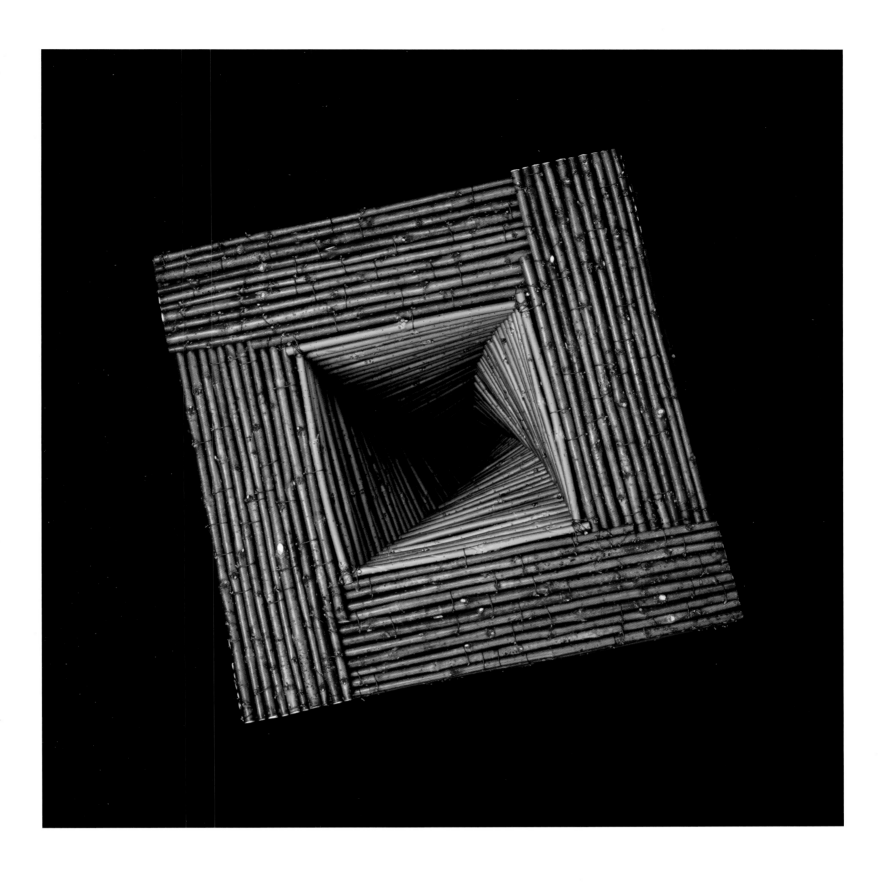

Left: A yard-high arch of stacked *Coccoloba uvifera* leaves is decorated with *Vanda* orchids.

Above: Autumnal stillness is captured in these fallen leaves from the park of Sint-Niklaas, which hang motionless from a branch like a sleeping bat.

SHISEIDO
TOKYO

In 2005 the Japanese cosmetics company Shiseido commissioned Ost to create the Christmas decorations for the Tokyo Ginza Shiseido Building, its headquarters in the commercial heart of Tokyo, built by the acclaimed postmodernist Catalan architect Ricardo Bofill. For Ost, this was the first of many collaborations with Shiseido. He remains grateful to the company for trusting him completely with that first commission, giving him both the freedom and the means to let his creativity flow. He designed floral artworks that responded to the architecture of the building–which, like his work, organically established bridges between East and West.

Left: Berries of the rare Korean *Smilax china* pour from a sculptural structure of green cornus.

Above: In 2005, for Shiseido's Christmas exhibition in the Imperial Hotel in Tokyo, Ost created this prickly little cushion, or bird's nest, of cornus branches decorated with *Gloriosa* lilies.

Following pages: *Asahi,* the rising sun, is constructed from red and green cornus with berries of *Smilax china.*

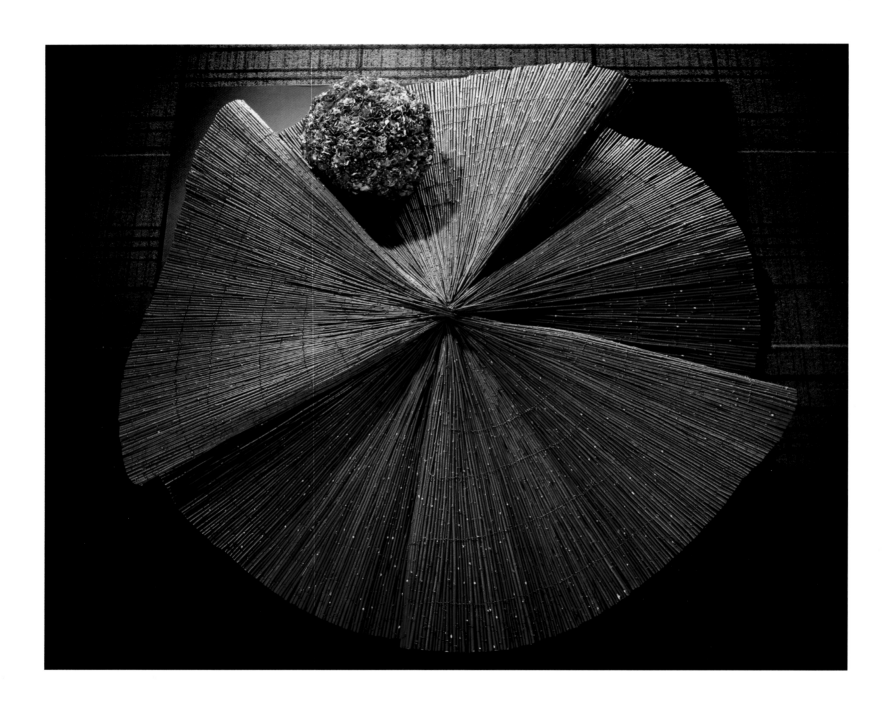

Above: Woven cornus and a sphere of bound
hortensia leaves constitute a technical tour
de force.

Right: Green berries of *Fatsia japonica*
slice into a circle of red cornus.

Left: An elegant waterfall of rose petals and an *Aspidistra* leaf hang from the ceiling of the top-floor restaurant.

Above: A floral design with cornus branches occupies one of the building's display cabinets.

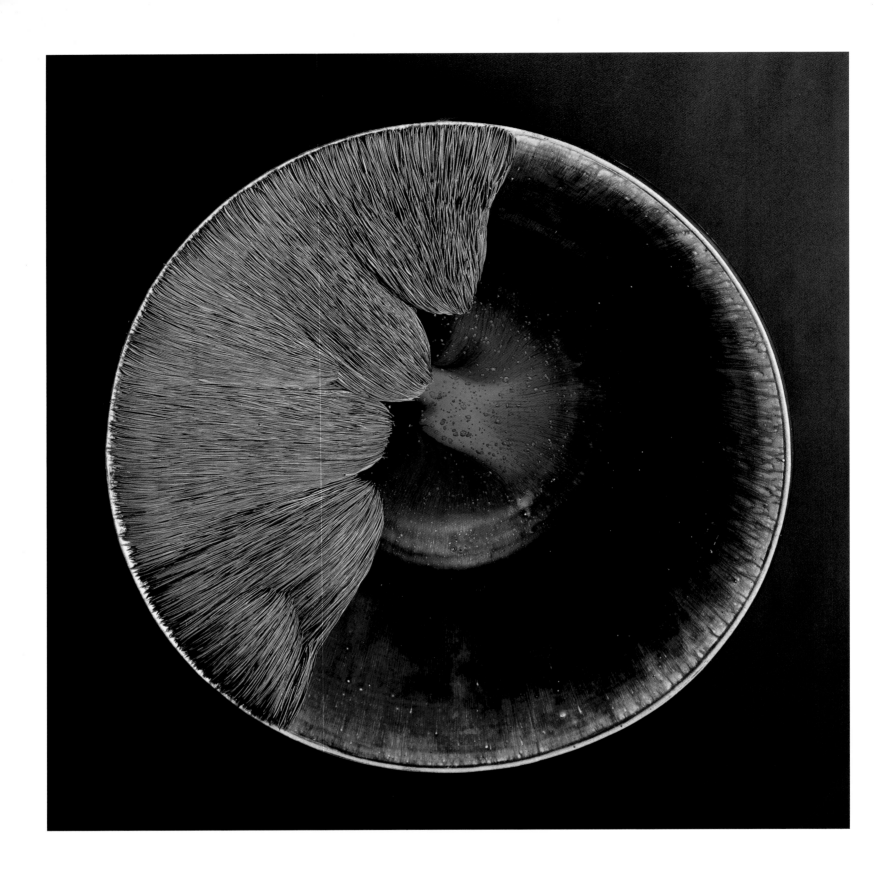

Above and right: Two minimalist compositions utilizing the leaves of *Magnolia grandiflora* create a perfect symbiosis with unique vases by the Japanese master ceramicist Ken Matsuzaki.

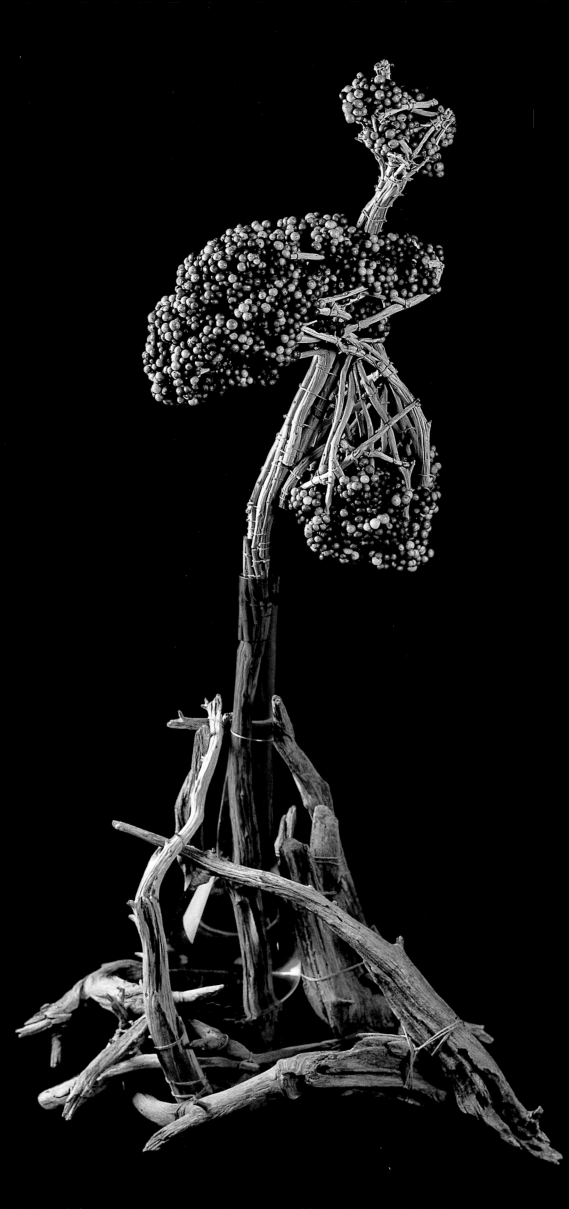

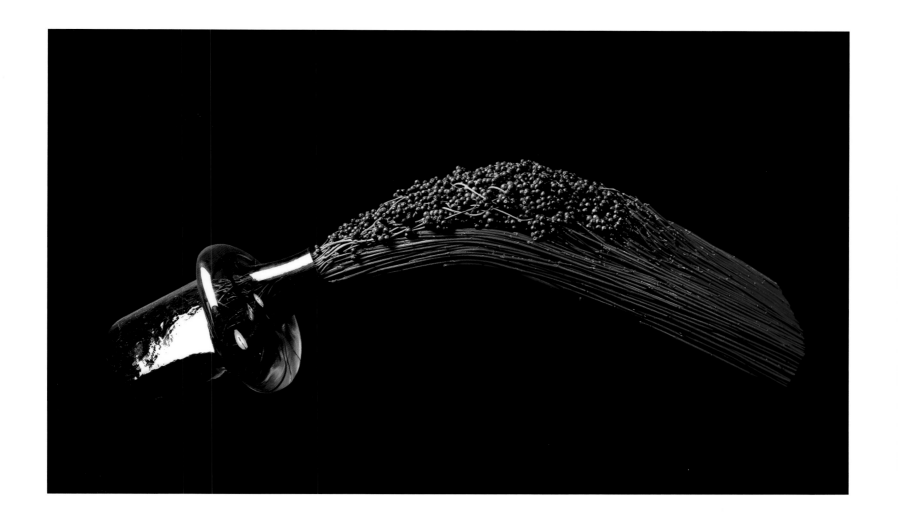

SŌGETSU PLAZA
TOKYO

In 2005 Ost was the first Westerner invited by the distinguished Sōgetsu School of ikebana for an exhibition in Sōgetsu Plaza at the headquarters of the Sōgetsu Foundation in Tokyo. The architect Kenzō Tange designed the building. Sōgetsu Plaza, at the entrance, is a masterwork by the Japanese-American sculptor Isamu Noguchi. In 1977, at the request of Sofu Teshigahara, founder of the Sōgetsu School, Noguchi created the Ò Tengoku Ó, or Heavenly Garden, a monumental contemporary interpretation of a traditional Japanese rock garden–a space used for exhibitions and displays.

Left and above: Everything starts with the form and the color of the vases in these compositions of branches and blue-purple porcelain berries.

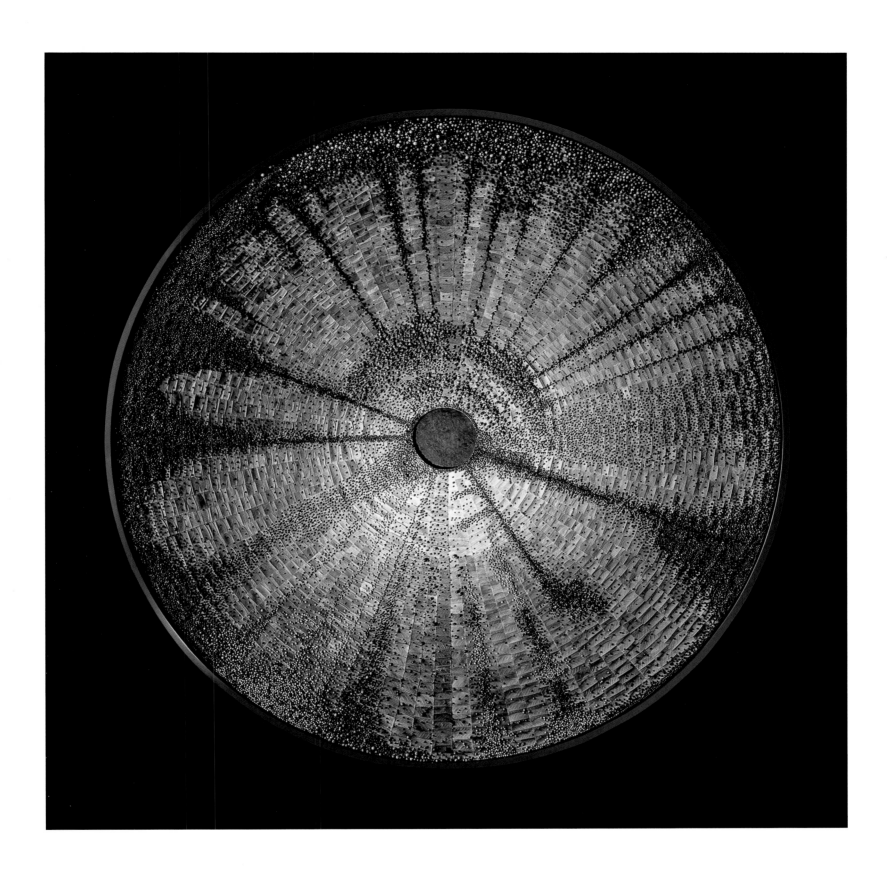

Left and above: Blue-purple porcelain
berries are attached to woven leaf
skeletons of *Magnolia grandiflora*.

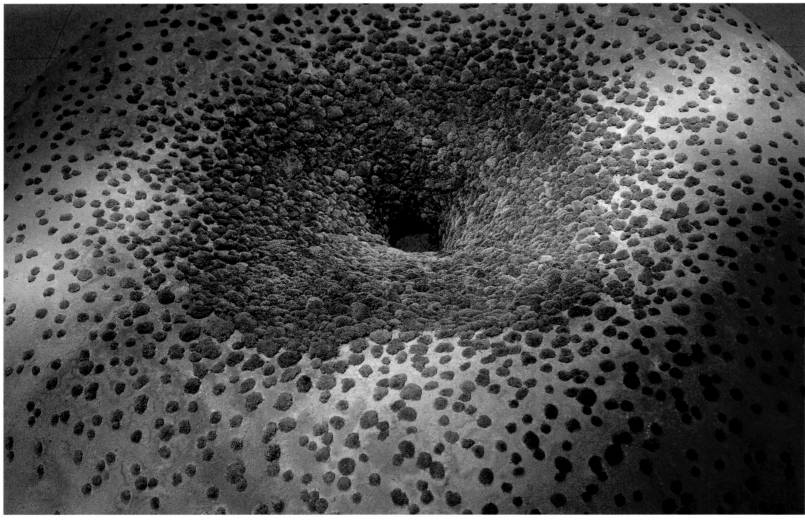

Flower decoration as spatial art: above left, porcelain berries, stuck one by one, on floral foam and set on top of a limestone sculpture by Isamu Noguchi; below left, a crater with the ash of *Prunus serrulata*

'Amanogawa' burned during the tea ceremony, covered in tufts of *Leucobryum glaucum*; and above, a mysterious sculpture with saffron-colored buds of the empress tree, *Leucobryum glaucum*.

Following pages: Pumpkins from the garden of the late EU commissioner Karel Van Miert form an impressive drystone wall.

MARSHALL FIELD'S
FLOWER SHOW
MINNEAPOLIS, MINNESOTA

In 2006, for the annual spring exhibition of the department store Marshall Field's (now Macy's) in Minneapolis, Ost created, with a team of Japanese assistants, a Japanese-like spring landscape with blossoming cherries and tulips.

Left: An installation representing the arrival of spring, with a river of camellia leaves and flowers, is inspired by both the Mississippi River and the Drowned Land of Saeftinghe.

Above: A spring landscape with blossoming cherry trees, azaleas, and tulips is topped with a wood structure in the shape of a Japanese fan.

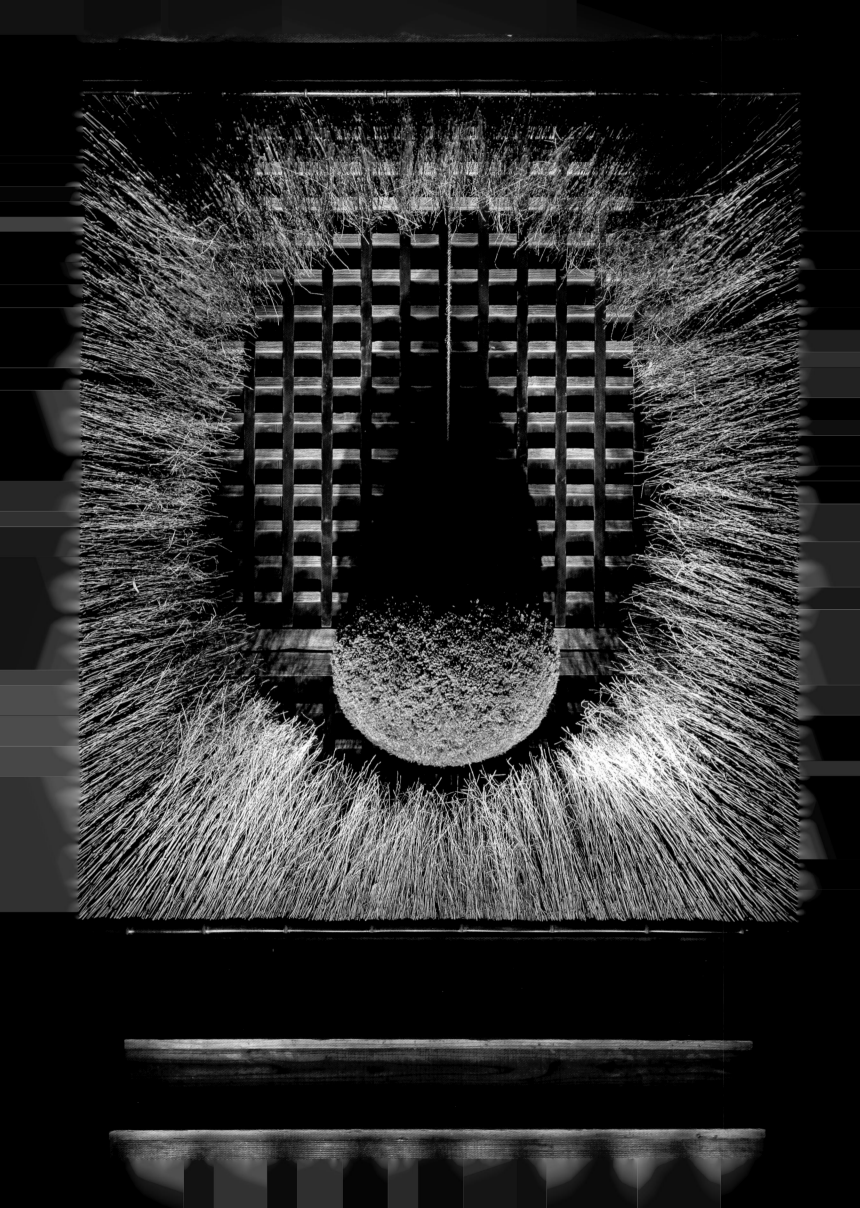

AUTUMN, TŌ-JI
KYOTO

The Tō-ji is a revered shrine of Shingon Buddhism and one of Kyoto's main tourist attractions. The complex has been a UNESCO World Heritage Site since 1994. Tō-ji was built in 796, when Kyoto became the capital of Japan. The current buildings date to the fifteenth, sixteenth, and seventeenth centuries. In November 2006, Ost held an exhibition there on the occasion of the 1,200th anniversary of the return of the founder of Shingon Buddhism, Kōbō Daishi, or Kūkai, from China. Ost exhibited in the Kanjoin, the ceremonial building that is reserved for the priests and normally closed to the public—an exceptional honor.

Left and above: Ost transformed the outer windows of the Kanjoin, which remain permanently closed so that no light penetrates the temple, into a mystical artwork of bamboo shoots and spheres of Japanese cedar.

Above and right: Two sober sculptures are made of bound cornus branches, bamboo, and the almost-black flowers of *Fritillaria camschatcensis,* in the dark shades of the wooden walls.

Following pages: An old barn door Ost discovered in the Japanese countryside inspired this yard-high sculpture of bamboo and red cornus.

SPRING, TŌ-JI
KYOTO

After his successful autumn exhibition in the famous temple of Tō-ji in 2006, Ost returned in March 2007 for a spring exhibition. He was once more welcomed into the Kanjoin, the ceremonial building normally reserved for the priests. For this display, Ost created a dialogue between the centuries-old wooden floors, walls, and beams and the fresh colors of spring.

Left: Ost created this abstract bamboo sculpture for the front of the shrine, inspired by the architecture of the temple.

Above: This composition for the temple's closed windows symbolizes the end of winter and the arrival of spring.

Above: A spiral of *Leucobryum glaucum* and the flowers of Japanese butterbur, one of the first to blossom in spring, nestles in a circle of clay with the ash of cherry wood burned during the tea ceremony. The spiral represents death and rebirth.

Right: A sculpture of cushion moss takes on human size and biomorphic form.

Left and above: Ost created these two installations in the main hall of the Kanjoin from split bamboo decorated with the fresh greenery and exotic flowers of *Stemona japonica* and clematis.

Following pages: Human-size figures of green cornus seem to engage in a lively choreography.

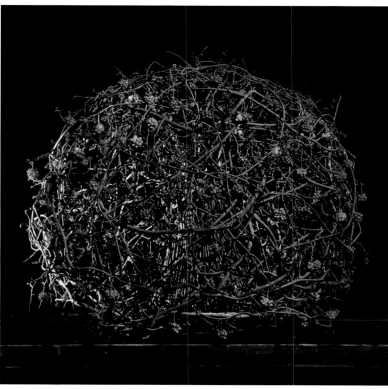

Clockwise from left: an elegant, fan-like shape of red cornus topped with a single Japanese tree peony, one of Ost's favorite flowers; a two-yard-high arch-shaped structure of red and green cornus; branches of red and green cornus forming a geometric structure; and buds, flowers, and berries of the rare Japanese andromeda, *Pieris japonica* 'Katsura,' woven together.

Two structures in which Ost pushed his technical limits to see how far he could go with a single element: above, the expressive power of bamboo with Japanese tree peonies; and right, a construction of black cornus is influenced by the architecture of the Golden Pavilion. Each *Arisaema* flower represents one of the monks.

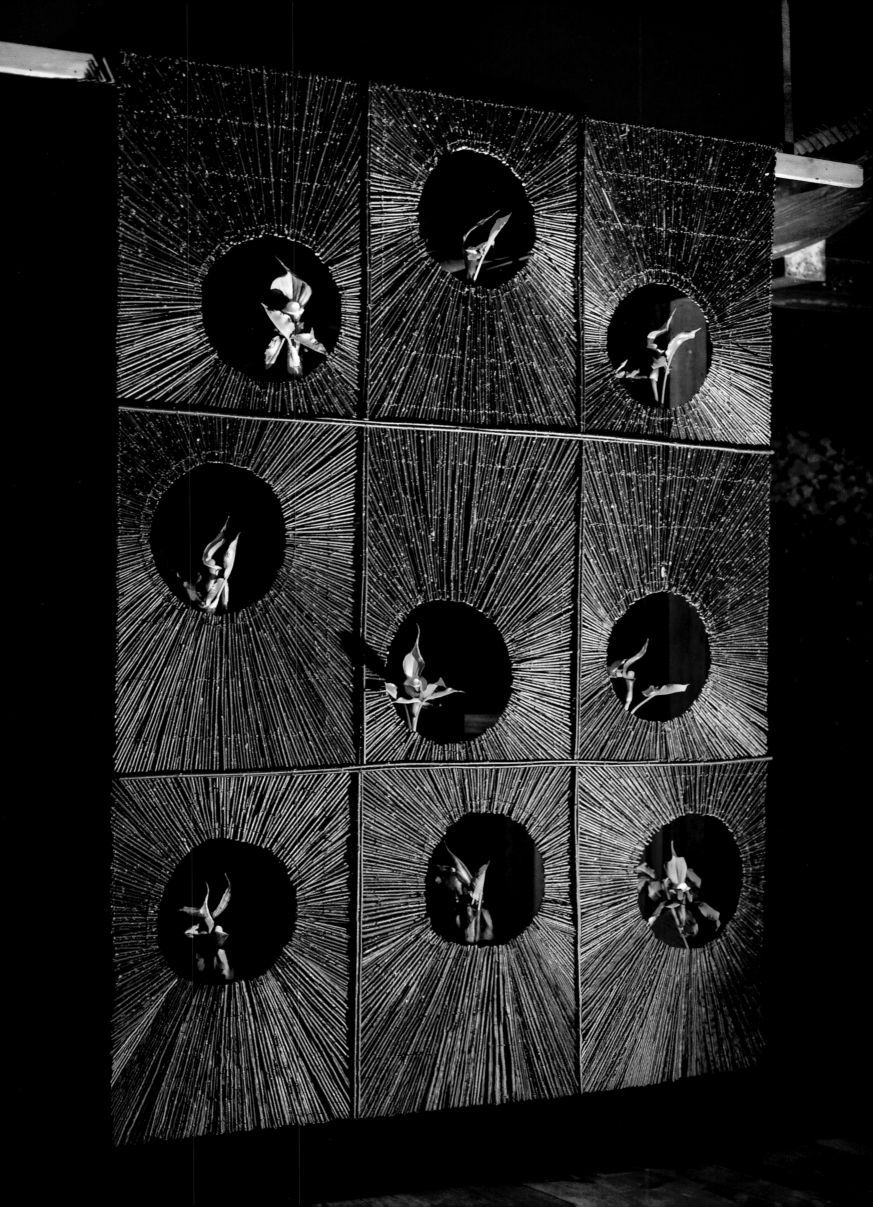

An ornamental frame of woven spindle
and cubes of *Aspidistra* leaves is reminiscent
of the motif in the wooden wall.

An interrupted circle of fluttering cherry
blossoms is suspended on nylon threads,
as an ode to spring.

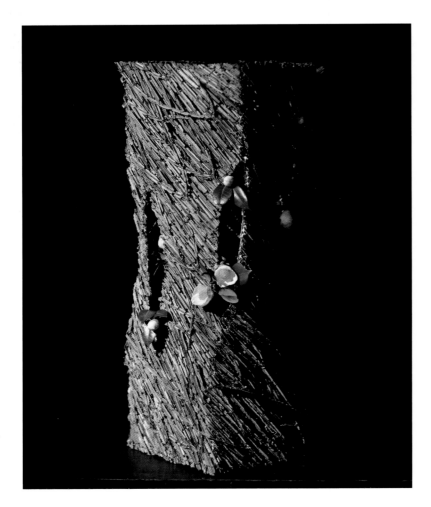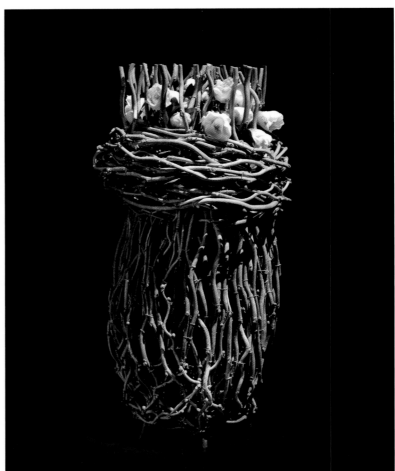

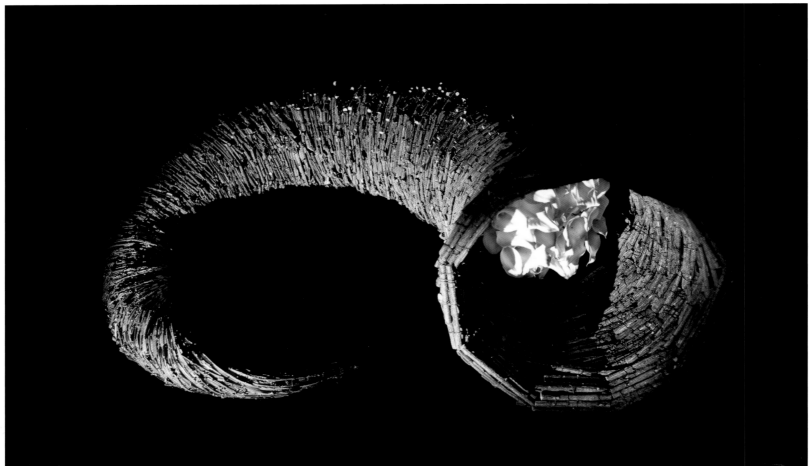

When plants rise from the dead, extinguished colors begin to glow again. Clockwise from top left: A structure approximately a yard high of woven branches of the Japanese spindle *Euonymus alatus* with the white *Camellia japonica;* woven branches of the common hazel, *Corylus avellana* 'Contorta,' with the white *Camellia japonica*; and a horn of Japanese spindle, *Euonymus alatus,* with white arums.

Right: The leaves of spring cherries from the park of Tō-ji and the rare curled white *Camellia japonica* come together to form a gateway to the gods.

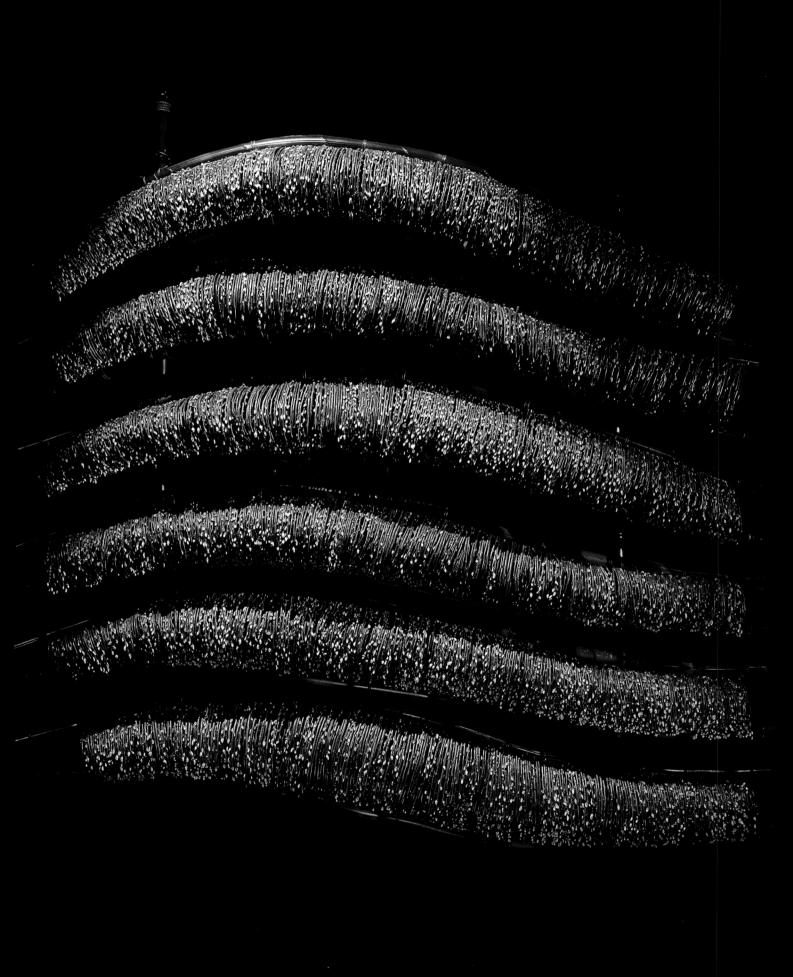

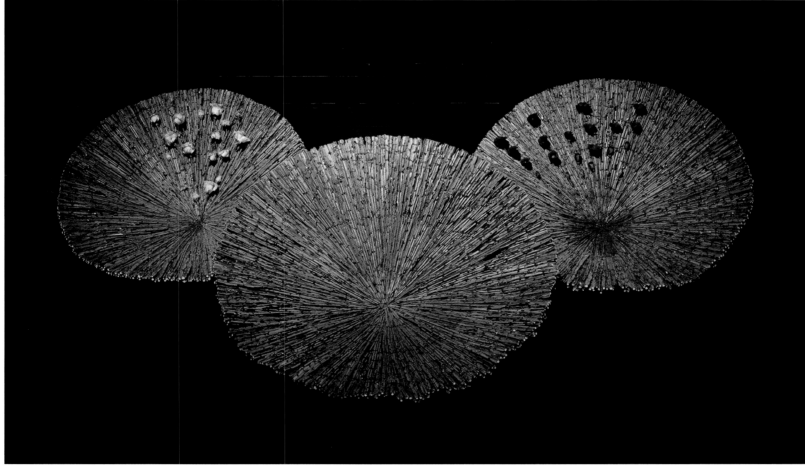

Left: A structure of willow branches woven with catkins on a frame of centuries-old charred bamboo was steam-bent into shape.

Above: These clay vases with the dark-red skunk cabbage, *Symplocarpus foetidus*, represent the monks of the temple.

Below: A few *Eustoma* flowers are scattered on circular structures of Japanese spindle. Each bloom represents one of the monks.

IMPERIAL HOTEL
TOKYO

The Imperial Hotel is located in the heart of Tokyo, next to the Imperial Palace, and is one of the oldest and most prestigious hotels in Japan. Built in 1890 at the request of influential Japanese aristocrats from the Imperial House of Japan, with the support of the Ministry of Foreign Affairs, it was intended to help accommodate the growing number of Western tourists. Ost has been invited here several times for the Christmas exhibition, in collaboration with Shiseido and Lexus.

Left: An ode to the rare Persian buttercup 'Charlotte,' a Japanese cultivar that is not readily available, on a structure of red cornus decorated with flowers of *Passiflora*.

Above: An opulent "classical" bouquet with some sixty different types of flowers and berries occupies a bronze vase by the Belgian company Domani.

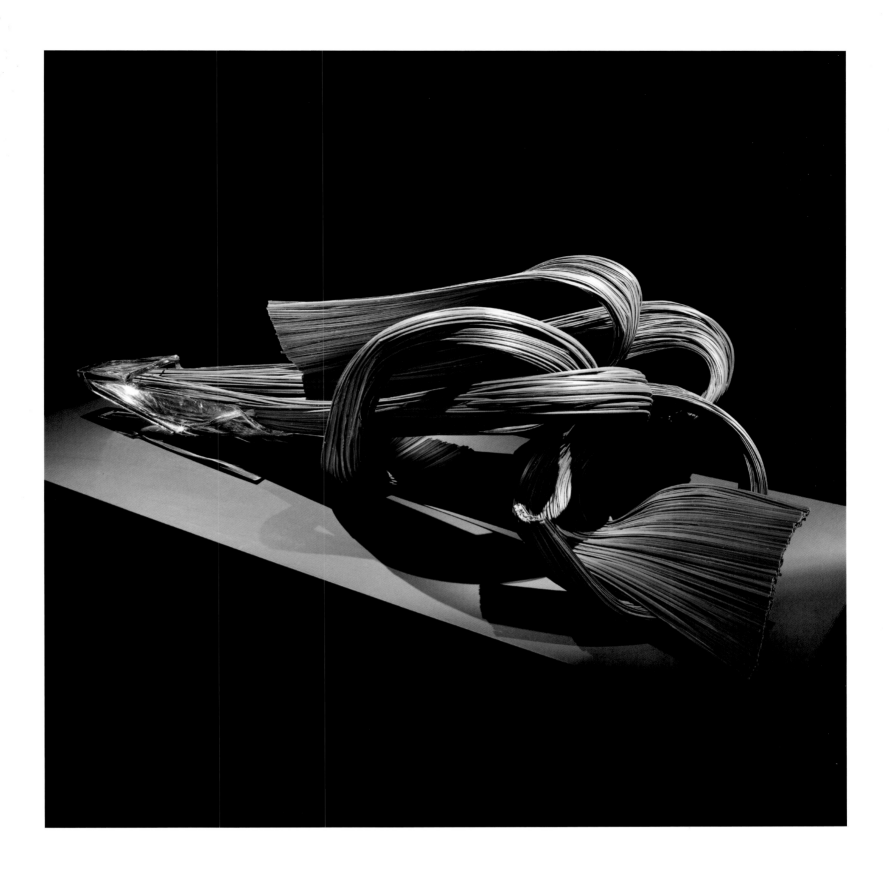

Two abstract figures that each measure more than a yard in length: *Aspidistra elatior* (left) and "massaged" steel grass (above).

Above: Berries of the heavenly bamboo, *Nandina domestica*, protrude from a sphere almost a yard in diameter composed of split and woven charred bamboo.

Right: A minimalist bouquet includes steel grass and the red berries of *Ilex verticillata*.

Following pages: A single budding *Hippeastrum* flower sits on an elegant fan of red cornus.

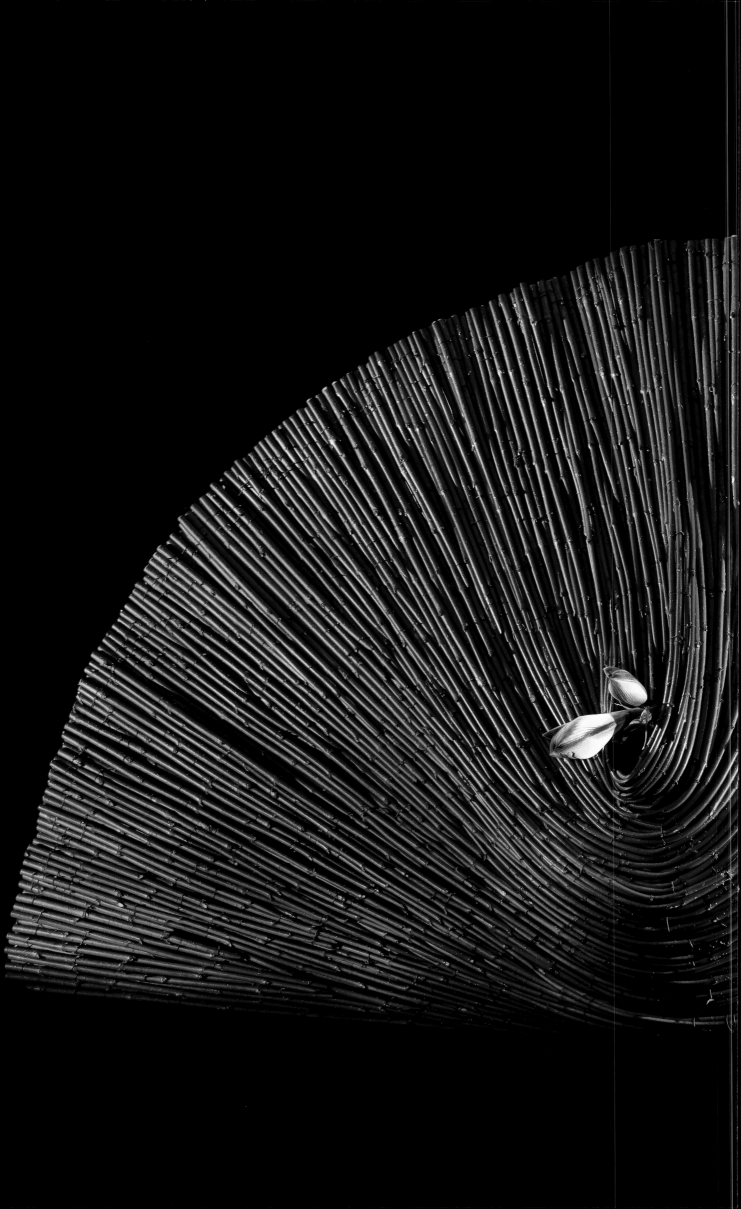

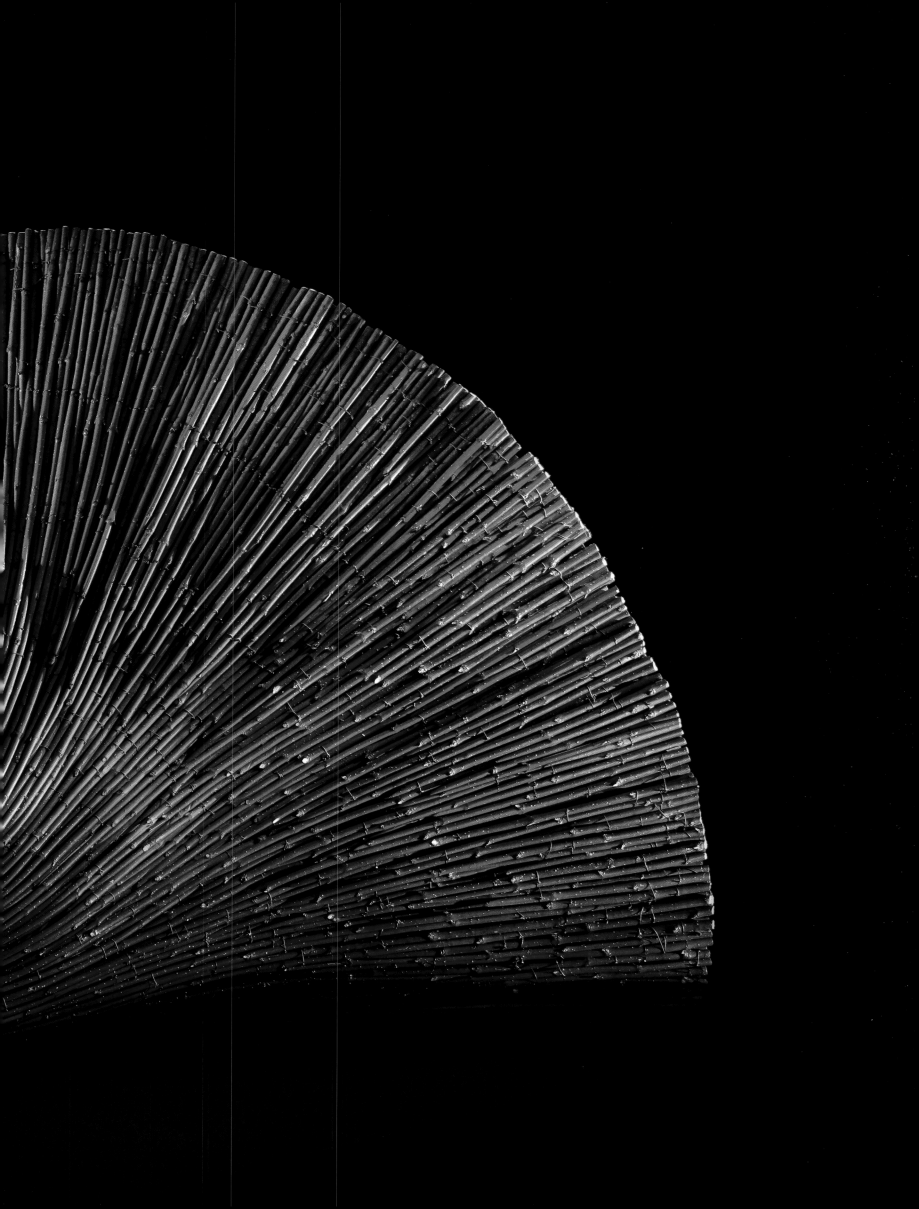

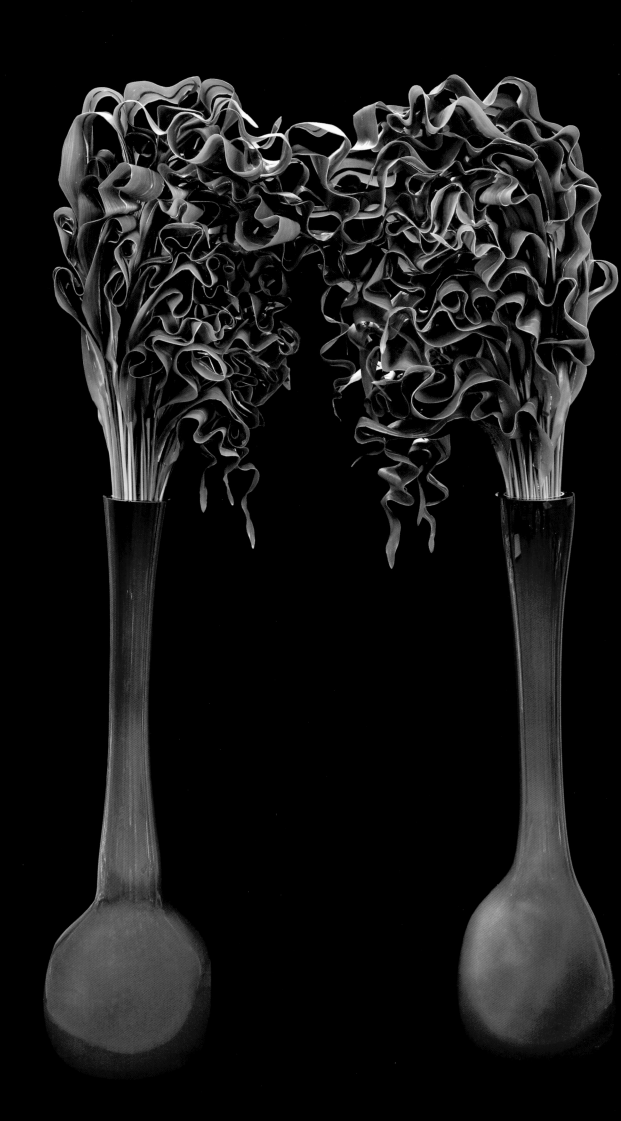

SOGO SHINSAIBASHI
OSAKA

In 2007 the department store Sogo organized the exhibition *Daniel Ost's Cosmos* at its recently renovated headquarters in Shinsaibashi, Osaka. Sogo was founded in 1830 by Ihei Sogo, a retailer of used kimonos, and grew into one of the most important Japanese department store chains, with branches throughout Asia and in various European capitals. The company reorganized in 2000 in the wake of financial difficulties, and the Osaka shop is now owned by Daimaru.

These and the following pages show a number of examples of Ost's artistic imagination and technical mastery. To make each of these restrained and seemingly simple creations, vegetal material is extracted from its context and transformed into a purified, abstract, yet sensual design in which only the essence is retained, in perfect symbiosis with the container.

Above: An architectural construction of bamboo with a rare species of Japanese clematis presides at the main entrance of Sogo Shinsaibashi Gallery.

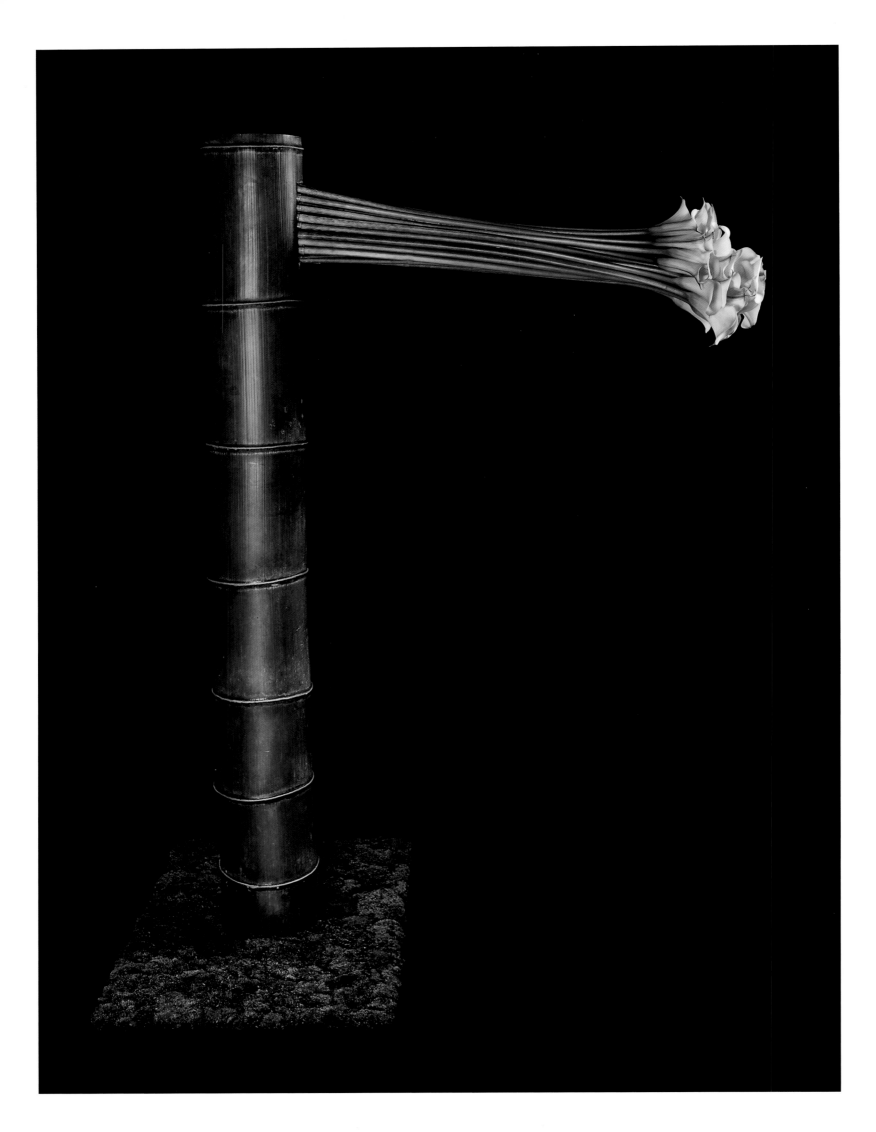

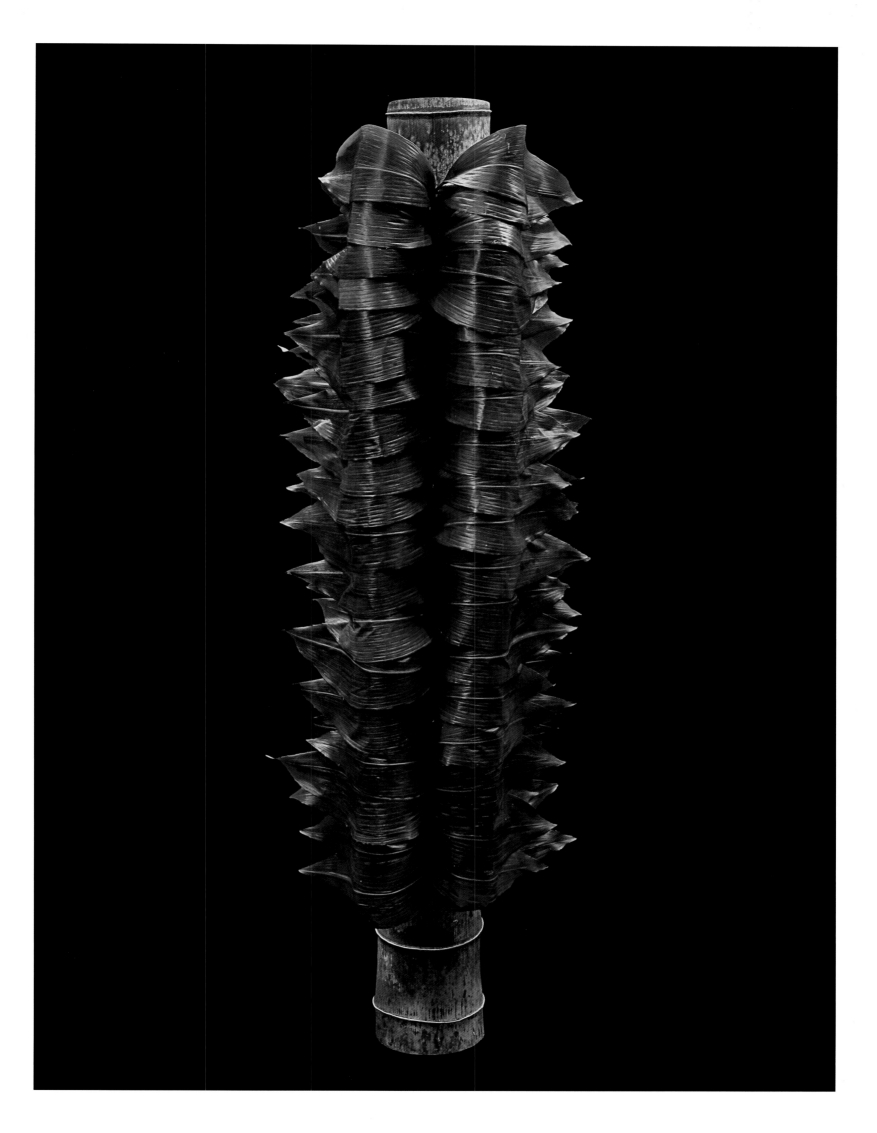

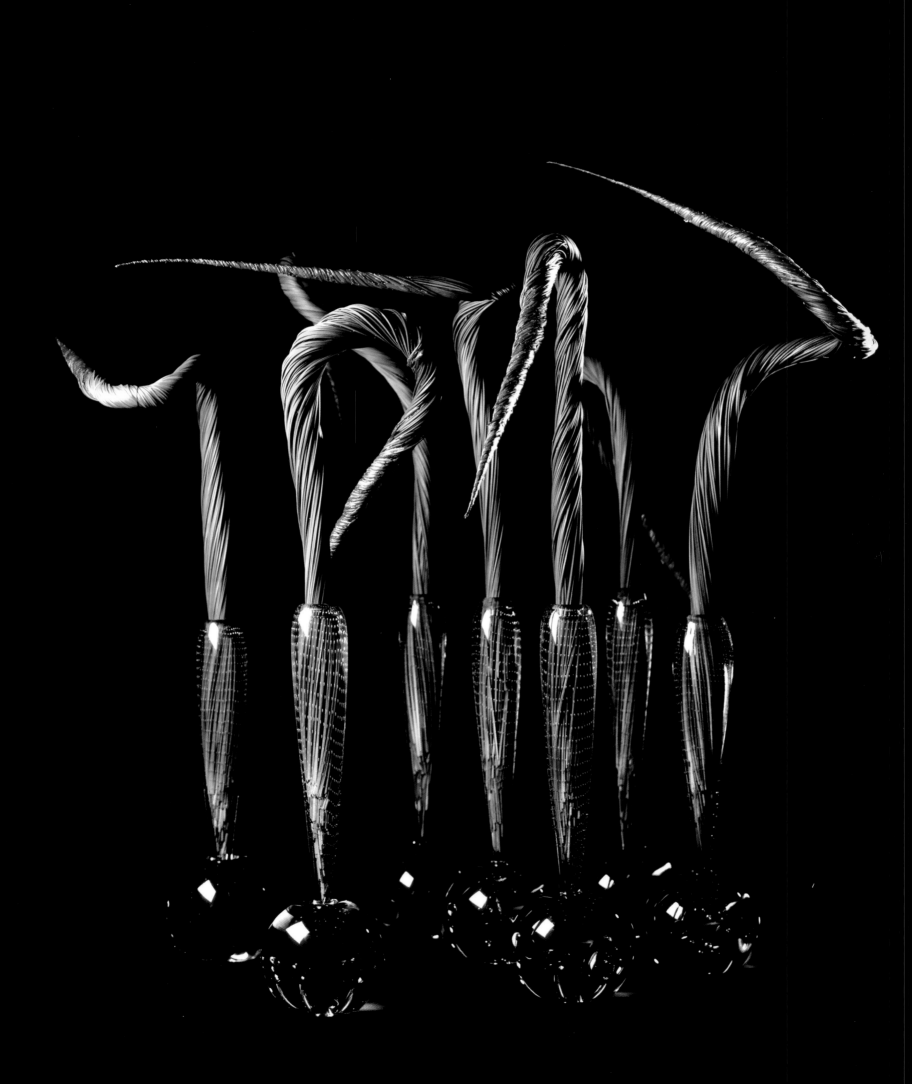

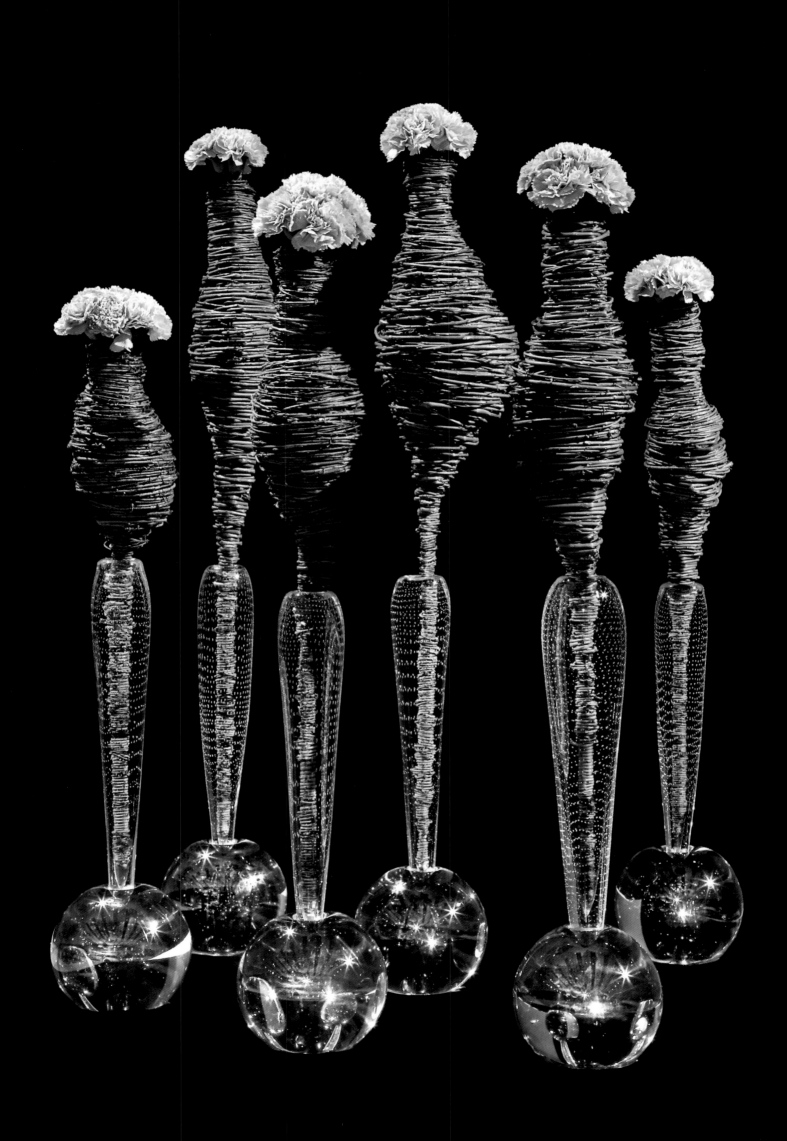

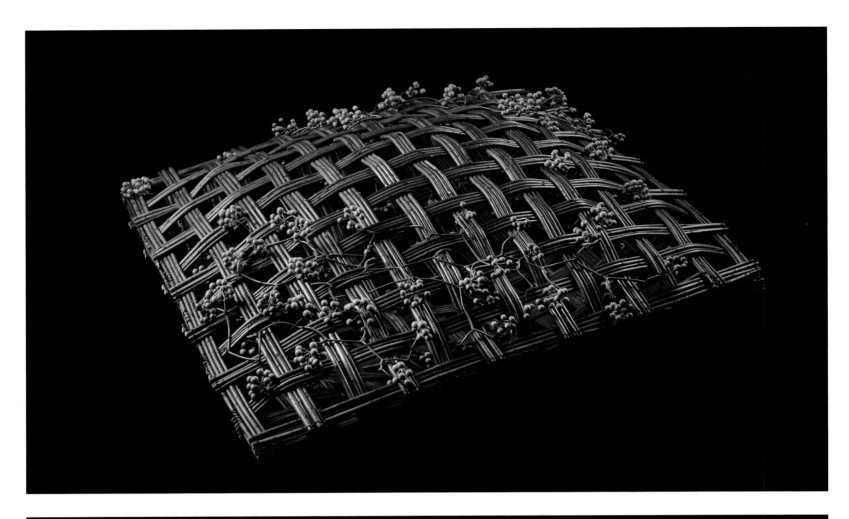

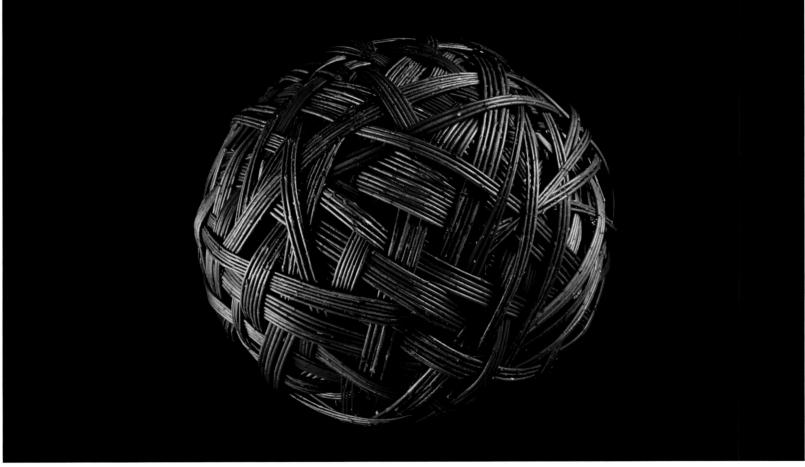

These four variations on a single theme all use woven and bound branches of red and green cornus. The top left example incorporates the unripe berries of *Smilax china,* and the top right sculpture includes the still-green flowers of the rare Chinese "happy tree," *Camptotheca acuminata.*

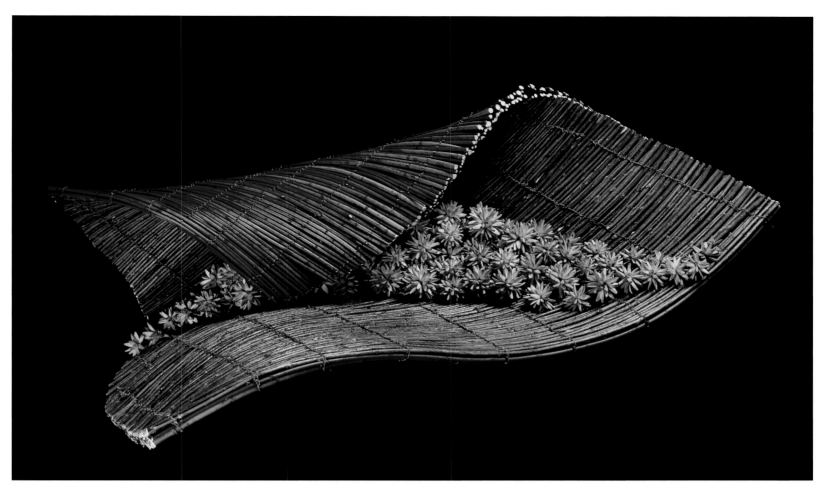

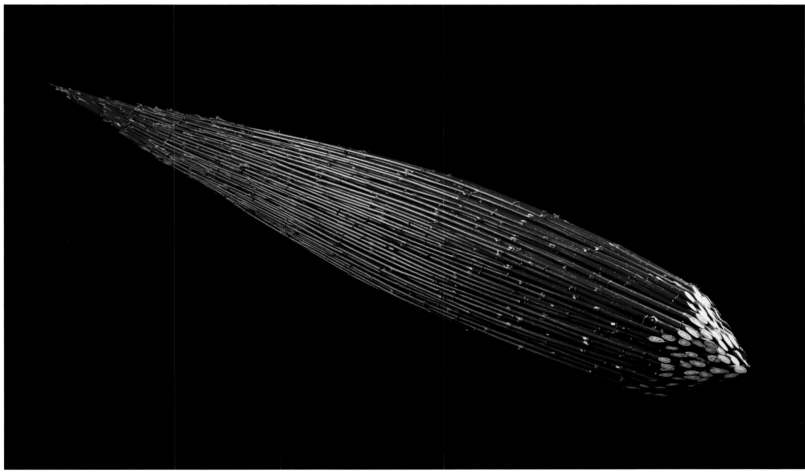

LANDCOMMANDERIJ ALDEN BIESEN

BILZEN, BELGIUM

Alden Biesen is one of the largest castles in the Euregio–the region between the Netherlands and Germany. Its history began in 1220 with the gift of a chapel and its accompanying grounds in Biesen to the German Order of Knights. In the fourteenth century, Biesen became a province whose administrative seat was the Alden Biesen Landcommanderij. The castle's glory days lasted from the sixteenth to the eighteenth century, during which time it became the luxury residence it is today. During the French Revolution, Alden Biesen was private property. After a devastating fire in 1971, the buildings were sold by the Belgian state, and brilliantly restored. Today Alden Biesen is a multipurpose cultural center with an international reputation.

Left: In 2009 Ost constructed a maze of laurel trees around a fountain of roses that adorned the main courtyard of Alden Biesen.

Above: For a flower arrangement event in the Alden Biesen Landcommanderij in 2005, Ost decorated the main courtyard with a sphere of red roses resembling a sun setting over ocean waves.

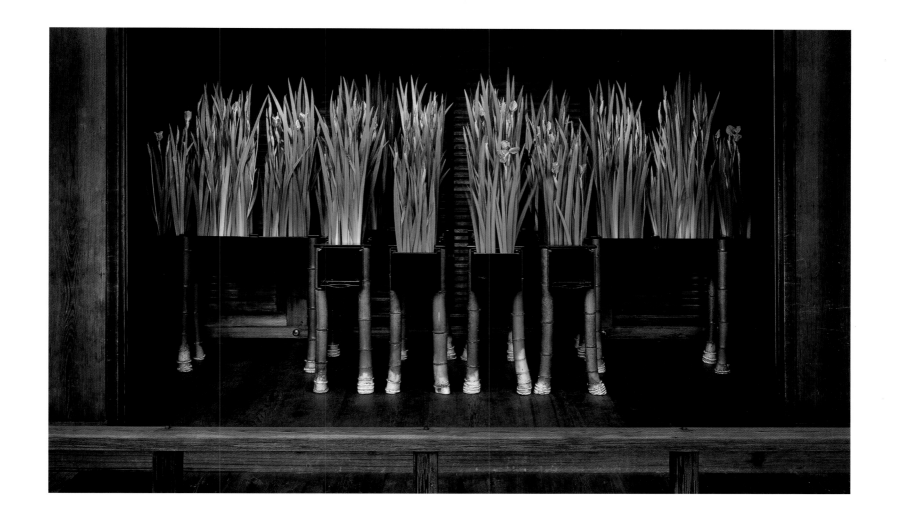

KINKAKU-JI
KYOTO

Kinkaku-ji, the Temple of the Golden Pavilion, in the beautiful gardens of Rokuon-ji, is one of the best-known temples in Kyoto. Covered in gold leaf, the Zen temple was built in the fourteenth century by Shogun Ashikaga Yoshimitsu. It is one of the most remarkable buildings in Japan and a UNESCO World Heritage Site. The pavilion was set on fire by a monk in 1950 but rebuilt several years later. The structure, which houses relics, is not accessible to the public. In spring 2009, Ost became the first Westerner to create an exhibition in the temple and the surrounding gardens.

Left: A circle of cherry blossoms sits on the raked stones in the Zen garden, with the Golden Pavilion in the background. Together with the triangle and the square, the circle forms the basis of Japanese geometry and symbolizes Japanese culture.

Above: A spring composition with *kakitsubata,* or Japanese irises, occupies custom containers of lacquerware with legs of bamboo.

Above and right: Modest organic
and anthropomorphic sculptures
of red cornus stand in the Zen garden.

Left: A human-size sculpture of green cornus is paired with the rare golden-colored *tsubaki,* or *Camellia japonica.*

Above: A yard-high geometric structure of expensive split bamboo has been specially treated to remain green forever.

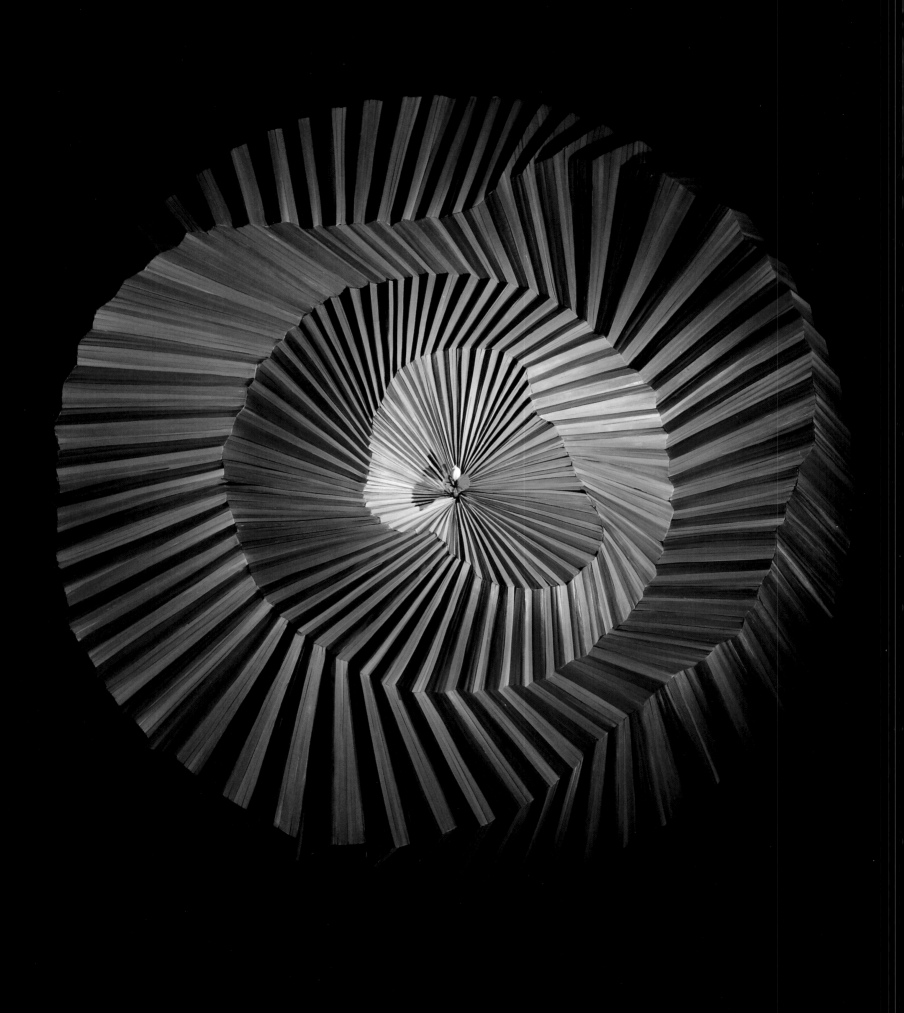

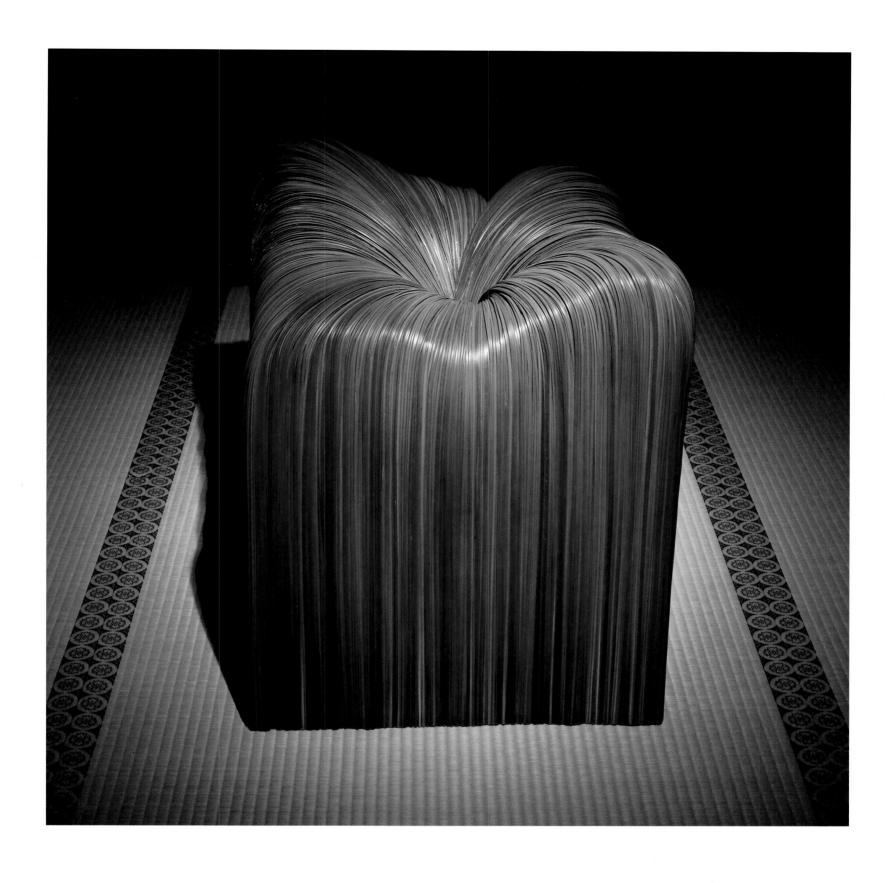

Left: By folding leaves according to a traditional origami technique, a type of shrine—representing the aureole of the sun—emerges for a rare Japanese orchid.

Above: This design of steel grass on tatami seems simple but was technically demanding.

Above: A yard-high composition with various species of clematis in bamboo vases.

Right: A modest, almost mystical tableau with small *Fritillaria* flowers and more than twelve thousand branches of steel grass is situated in specially made pots of Japanese lacquerware and old bamboo. A wooden disk from a five-hundred-year-old walnut tree is in the background.

This clay panel with camellia flowers
ranging from bud to full blossom
is based on a baroque drawing
of a seventeenth-century art room
with tile in Delft blue. It is intended
to represent the force of a black
hole from which nothing can escape.

An undulating tableau in split bamboo
represents the moon.

Two tableaux: Left, porcelain-colored callas in a cocoon of red cornus; and above, light-pink roses as precious relics.

Above: A room-size installation of green
bamboo features clematis flowers and more.

Right: *Aspidistra* leaves hold two bamboo
stalks in an intimate embrace.

LAURENT-PERRIER
TOKYO AND PARIS

Over the years, Ost has worked regularly with the French champagne house Laurent-Perrier. In 2010 he created an elegant Cuvée Rosé garden on the roof terrace of the iconic Chanel building in Ginza, Tokyo, where the famed restaurant Beige, featuring the French chef Alain Ducasse, is located. On the occasion of the garden event "Jardins, Jardin" in the Jardin des Tuileries in Paris in 2007, Ost designed an ephemeral Grand Siècle garden, a flower fountain with white arums. These commissions occupy a position somewhere between flower design, land art, and garden architecture, and he devotes the greatest care to the smallest of details.

Left: A river of black Japanese rocks with islands of baby's tears, *Soleirolia soleirolii*, weaves its way between hills of cushion moss, *Leucobryum glaucum*.

Above: Ost created this moon garden with grass, moss, and pink verbena for the Cuvée Rosé garden of Laurent-Perrier.

Following pages: A five-yard-long cylindrical structure supports thousands of Japanese spring cherry flowers in glass test tubes attached to Plexiglas disks.

In the Grand Siècle garden in the Tuileries
in Paris, Ost installed a twenty-five-yard-long
flower fountain with 1,500 white arums and
high laurel trees in a bed of *Buxus* trimmed
in Japanese fashion.

An impressive installation with large Bruges
laurel trees in the cloister designed by the
Renaissance architect Andrea Palladio
on Isola di San Giorgio Maggiore, Venice.

Above: A breaking wave of steel grass with calla flowers evokes ancient Japanese prints.

Below: A flowing structure of red and green cornus is adorned with rare white and green *Gloriosa*.

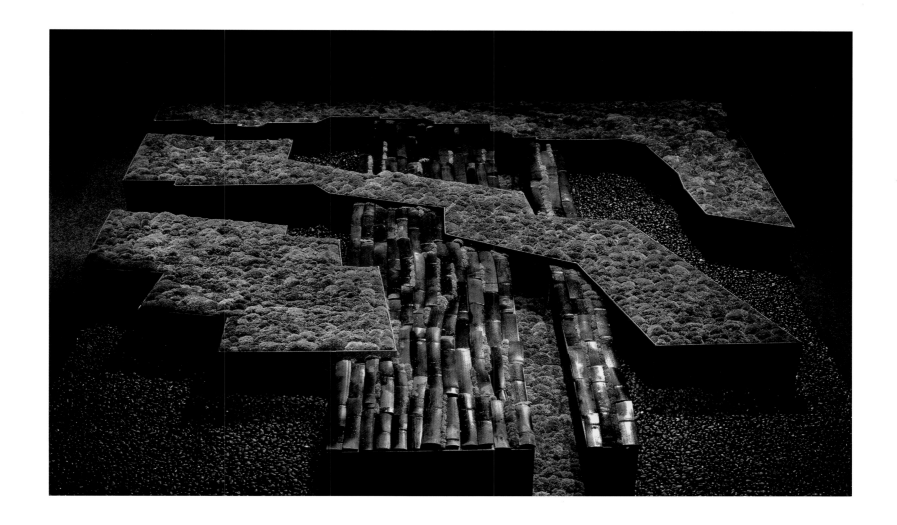

SEIBU IKEBUKURO
TOKYO

Seibu Ikebukuro is one of the largest department stores in Japan. The shopping complex includes a large food market, dozens of specialized fashion, cosmetics, and interior design shops, and various restaurants. In spring 2008 and 2010, Ost designed extensive exhibitions in the Seibu Gallery. In 2010 the exhibition *Daniel Ost: Flora Cosmos* made highly innovative use of French Baccarat crystal vases.

Above: This miniature landscape incorporates moss and charred bamboo; the latter is a traditional architectural material that protects a building from water and fire.

In variations on a theme, flowers and plants form a duality in shape and color with the vases by L'Anverre: above left, woven palm leaves; above right and below, folded and glued leaves of *Aspidistra elatior* 'Asahi,' or 'Rising Sun,' in reference to its white tip; and at right, steel grass with large peony-shaped buttercups.

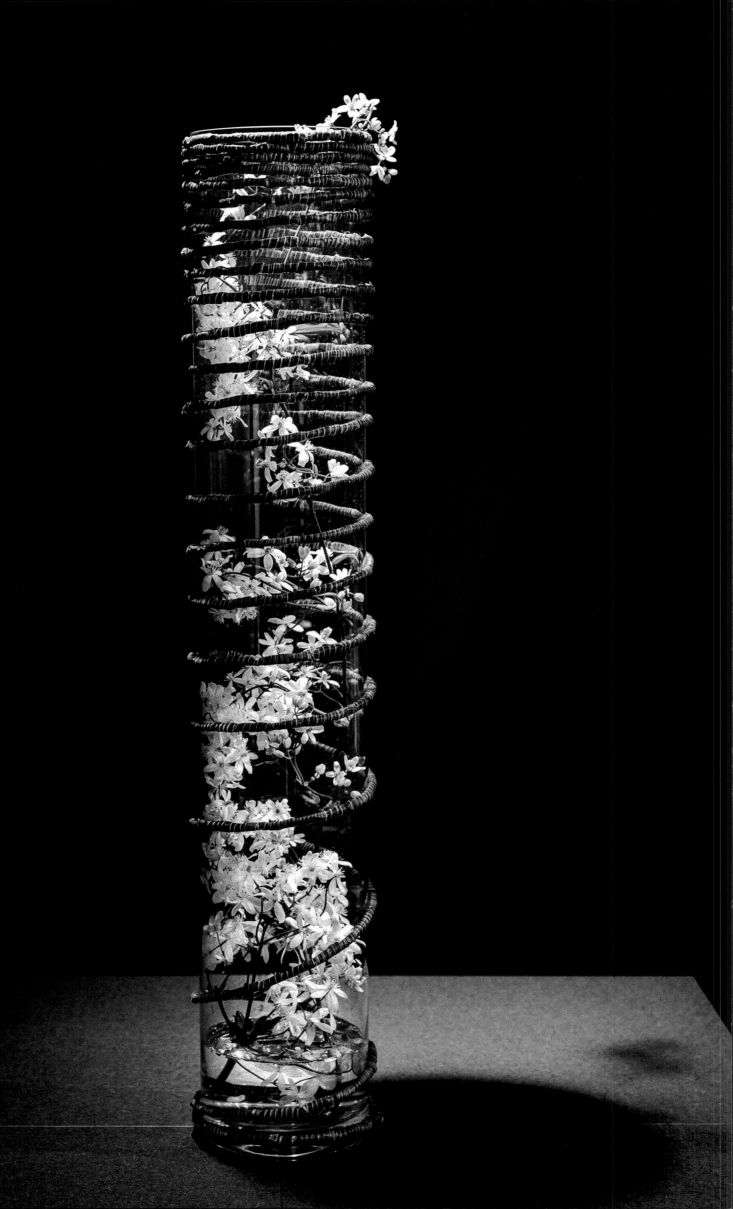

In more variations on a theme, flowers and plants form a unity of shape and color with their vases. Clockwise from left: A simple glass vase enveloped with steel grass and a wild Japanese clematis; a glass vase wrapped with red cornus; a screen of steel grass with a single white calla flower; a vase of willow branches with small lily flowers; and a composition of *Equisetum hyemale,* or scouring rush, with young fern shoots that are just unfurling.

Following pages: A minimalist composition of woven weeping willow branches incorporates the light-blue flowers of the South American *Oxypetalum caeruleum.*

Left: A blooming spiral of willow catkins complements the flowers of *Eustoma*.

Above: Needles of the Japanese longleaf pine, *Pinus palustris*, form the shape of a fan.

Following pages: In a display of technical mastery, the insides of the *Magnolia grandiflora* leaf are brought together with *Epidendrum* orchids in glass test tubes.

Above: A three-yard-long installation of willow shoots, with which Ost tests the flexibility of the material, is decorated with *Eustoma,* sweet peas, and ferns.

Right: A Persian buttercup is a prima ballerina in a crown of red cornus.

Above and right: Two remarkable
compositions with red cornus branches
in Baccarat vases represent Ost's
indefatigable search for the ultimate
combination of plant, flower, and vase.

Left: An organic sculpture brings together
the leaf of *Magnolia grandiflora* with striking
South American *Zygopetalum* orchids.

Above: An esoteric sculpture of steel
grass becomes creature-like with the
addition of a single cobra lily, *Arisaema*.

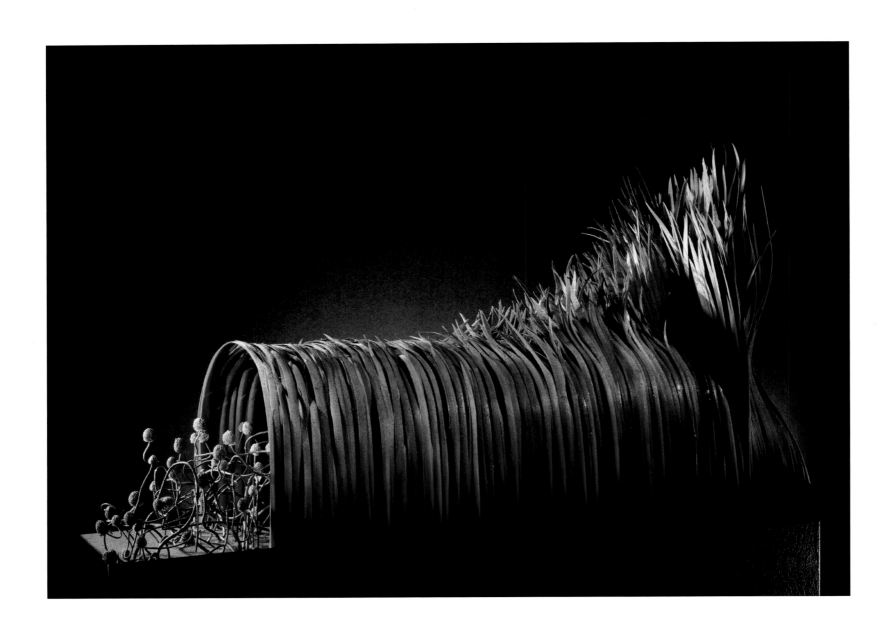

Above: A sculpture of "massaged" iris leaves is inhabited by the dancing buds of the twisting *Allium sativum* var. *ophioscorodon*.

Right: Two controlled compositions feature ginger stems with rare Japanese Venus slippers, *Paphiopedilum* (left), and steel grass with twisting *Allium sativum* var. *ophioscorodon* (right).

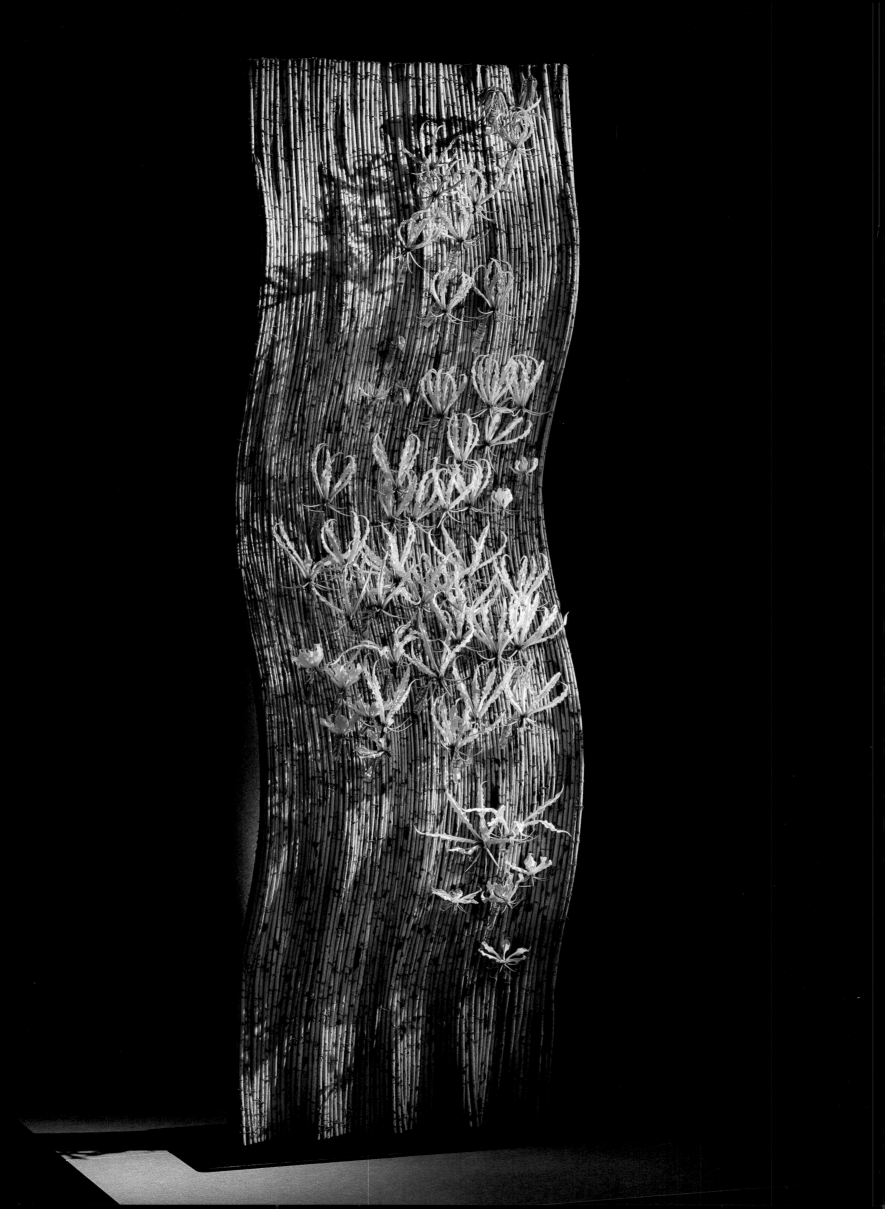

Left: A screen of braided cornus branches supports rare white *Gloriosa* lilies.

Above: In an example of the perfect relationship between vase and bouquet, very rare yellow *Lycaste* orchids decorate cornus branches in a crystal Baccarat vase.

Intimate sculptural works of twined weeping willow: above, with the flowers of *Lachenalia* and green clematis; and right, with green *Gloriosa* flowers.

Following pages: A forest of *Lachenalia* rests in a crater of cushion moss.

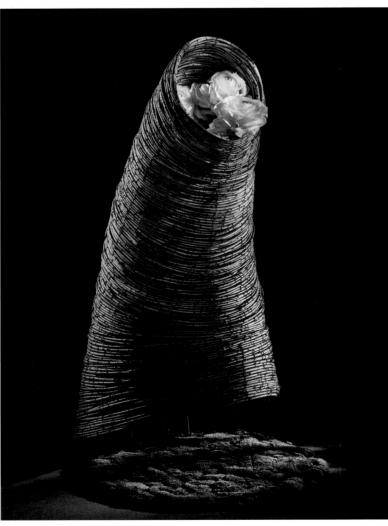

Left, clockwise from top left: Poppies—in bud, in bloom, and open—on a construction of willow with ivy leaves; a weave of curly willow decorated with green buttercups; gerberas and ivy tendrils in a handmade vase of yellow cornus; and a horn of woven yellow-green cornus with yellow Persian buttercups on a bed of moss.

Above: A Brueghelian bouquet presides in a bronze vase, created out of some eighty varieties of flowers and leaves.

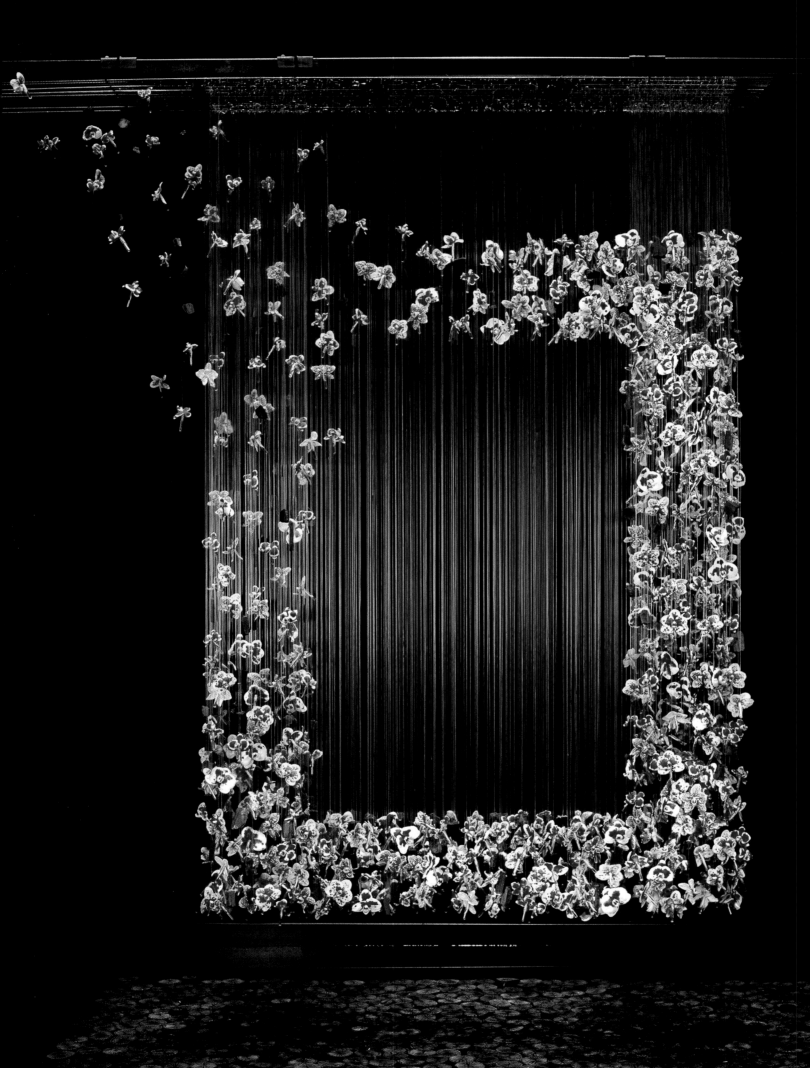

GHENT FLORALIES
GHENT, BELGIUM

The Ghent Floralies, which takes place every five years, is one of the most important flower exhibitions in the world. The show dates back to February 1809, when a few amateur horticulturists organized a small exhibition of fifty different plants, *Au Jardin de Frascati,* in the tavern on Ghent's Kouter Square. It was a time when wealthy squires and citizens were designing beautiful parks and building *orangeries* in which to practice their horticultural hobbies. Since then, the flower show has become a lavish showcase, a kind of fashion show, for the products of the Ghent flower industry and a forum where foreign growers can present their novelties. Over time, countless new plants have been introduced, such as camellias, orchids, begonias, and of course azaleas, still the pride of Ghent horticulture. In recent shows, a great deal of attention has been devoted to flower arrangement, with creations by leading flower designers presented much like museum pieces.

Left: A mysterious illusion for the Ghent Floralies in 2005 looks like perhaps it is raining orchids, or the flowers are breaking free of their tight frame.

Above: Ost won first prize in 2010 with this simple composition of a peacock plant, or *Calathea,* on a network of golden threads.

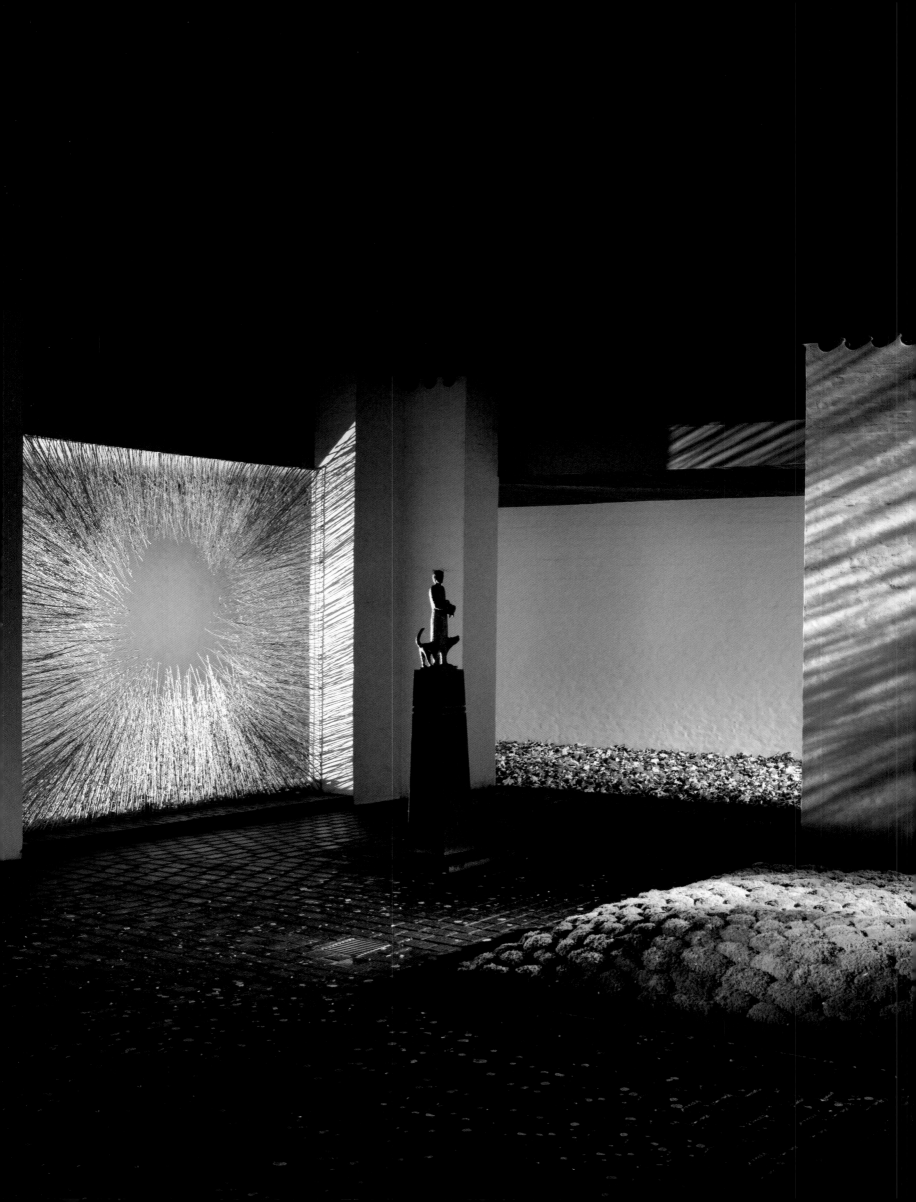

REFLECTION 775
ROOSENBERG ABBEY
WAASMUNSTER, BELGIUM

With the 2012 exhibition *Reflection 775* at Roosenberg Abbey in Waasmunster, Belgium, Ost returned to his roots. While working on his first book in 1989, he had knocked on the door of the Franciscan Sisters of Mary to ask if he could photograph his floral works in their timeless convent architecture designed by the Benedictine architect Dom Hans van der Laan—a dream for an artist with big plans but no money. Years later, when he heard that the roof of the abbey needed significant repairs—and that the abbey happened to be celebrating its 775th birthday—he wanted to give something back to the sisters and carried out a benefit exhibition to raise the necessary funds.

Left: A fiery aura of red cornus is offered to Saint Francis, patron saint of the abbey.

Above: A creation of split bamboo decorated with orchids and *Gloriosa* looks like a fountain installed in the cloister's pond.

Ost is a master at dialoguing with space.
Above, a bamboo "organ" with multicolored
Vanda orchids adds an element of levity to
the sober architecture of the abbey chapel.

At right, a wave of split bamboo with
Vanda orchids flows down the stairs,
with umbrellas to symbolize the abbey's
leaking roof.

Left: An enigmatic sculpture features a handmade bamboo vase in the form of a half-moon with a single chrysanthemum, against the background of a centuries-old walnut disk.

Above left: *Vanda* orchids decorate a pillar of dried autumn leaves.
Above right: Ost evokes Saint Francis with a single *Vanda* orchid in a Japanese vase of split bamboo.

Following pages: An impressive composition brings together the leaves and some hundred buds of the peace lily, *Spathiphyllum*.

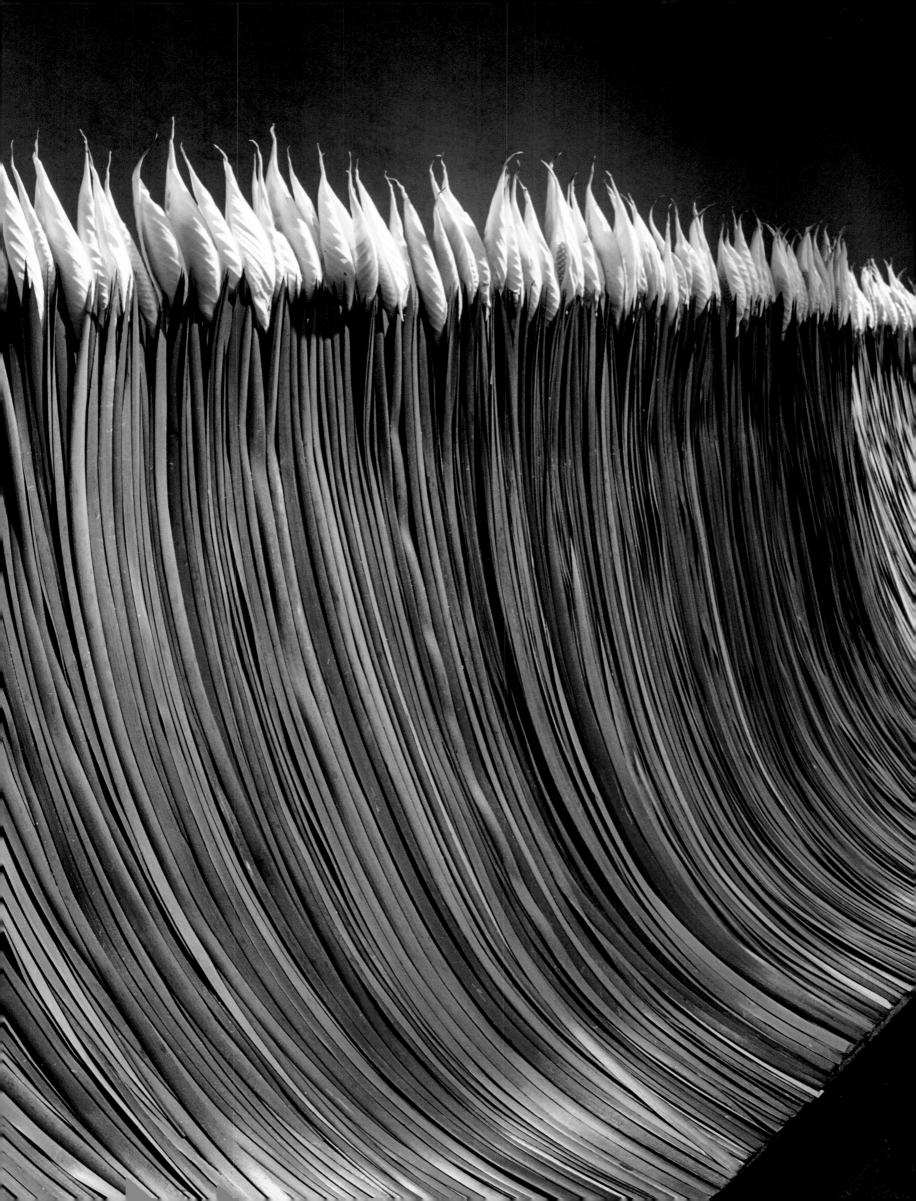

IZUMO-TAISHA

IZUMO

Izumo-taisha is one of the oldest and most treasured Shinto shrines in Japan. Legend has it that Ōkuninushi-no-kami, the god of marriage and good relations and the creator of Japan, emerged from the sea at this very spot to build a temple. According to tradition, the gods are born here and return each year in the autumn. The current main building was built in the pure Taisha-zukuri style. Its original architecture dates back to 1744, before the rise of Buddhism in Japan, although there was already a temple here in the seventh century. Every sixty years, the temple is renovated as part of the *sengu,* a ritual to renew and reinforce the bond with the gods. The works Ost created for this exhibition in 2013 responded to the special architecture and the centuries-old history of the shrine, as well as the flowers and plants from the Izumo region.

Left: "Incense plumes" of woven bamboo stand before the entrance of the shrine.

Above: A sculpture of straw—influenced by the traditional *shimenawa,* or rice straw rope—and Japanese tree peonies.

Following pages: All of the materials for this room-size sculpture, made with the needles of the Chinese Kaizuka juniper on legs of moss-covered peach wood, came from the temple garden. The needles were attached, one at a time, to floral foam. The form was inspired by antique paintings in the temple.

Left: A cloud of cedar needles, *Cryptomeria japonica*, floats above a boat-shaped construction covered in cedar bark and filled with moss, a reference to the genesis of the temple.

Above: A thirteen-yard-long "smoke plume" of Japanese cedar needles undulates from the kitchen of the temple complex.

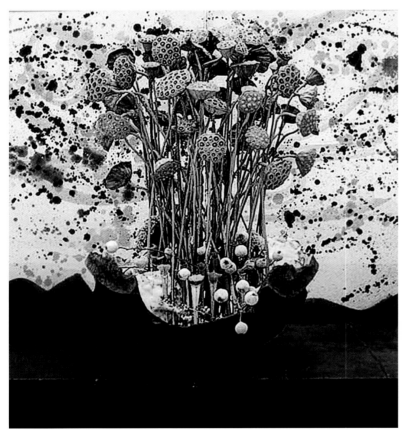

Above: A room-size structure of bamboo with blue clematis flowers and the capsules of the lotus flower–considered sacred in Buddhism–beautifully complements lotus prints by the designer Mutsuko Yawatagaki, who uses a centuries-old paper technique.

Below left and right: The delicate capsules of the lotus flower are ideal for this smaller composition.

Right: Detail of the bamboo with blue clematis flower structure.

The head coverings of the monks of Izumo-taisha
inspired this vegetal sculpture made with the
needles of the longleaf pine, *Pinus palustris*.

This sculpture of woven veneer wood of the
Japanese cedar with *Phalaenopsis* orchids
references the building's architecture.

THE MOST BEAUTIFUL FLOWER STORY

MIYAZAKI

In spring 2015, Ost was invited for *The Most Beautiful Flower Story* in Miyazaki, a popular holiday destination on the subtropical eastern coast of the island of Kyushu, Japan. He exhibited in the Seagaia Convention Center, part of the Miyazaki Prefectural Museum of Nature and History, and in Miyazaki-jingū, the city's oldest temple. This Shinto shrine, whose origins are said to date back 2,600 years, is dedicated to Emperor Jimmu, the mythical first emperor of Japan and a direct descendant of the gods. The current temple of cedar wood was constructed in the twelfth century and has been rebuilt over the years.

Left and above: Giant bamboo sculptures
symbolize the upward movement
of humankind toward the gods.

ŌHARA RESIDENCE & MUSEUM
KURASHIKI

With its bridges, canals, and traditional buildings, Kurashiki, a picturesque and well-preserved town from the Edo period, is sometimes called the Venice of Japan. Ost exhibited here in spring 2015 in the beautiful Ōhara Residence, with its formerly imperial rooms, and at the Ōhara Museum of Art. Built in 1930 by the textile magnate Magosaburō Ōhara, this museum holds an impressive collection of Western art accumulated by Kojima Torajiro, who studied at the Royal Academy of Fine Arts in Ghent, Belgium. Fumihito, Prince Akishino and his daughter, Princess Kako of Akishino, attended the opening, an exceptional honor for a Westerner.

Left, above, and following pages: The garden in the Ōhara Residence combines 1,500 square feet of moss from the mountains with tiles of the imperial residence. *Primula* grows between the moss hills. The colors of the buildings mix with the shades of the flowers floating in the Plexiglas vessels: peonies, buttercups, chrysanthemums, anemones.

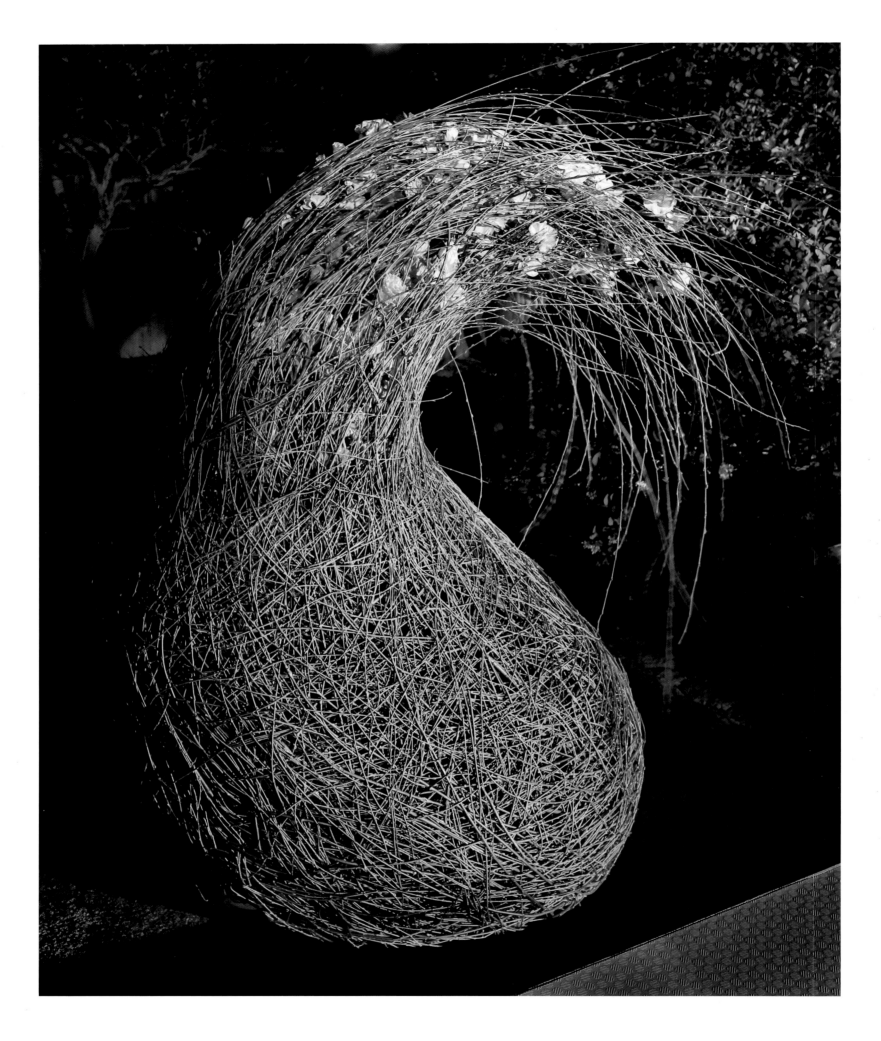

Above: A structure measuring more than two yards high combines woven weeping willow with the flowers of the rare *Lathyrus odoratus* 'Antique Brown.'

Right: A bouquet nearly five yards high resides in a centuries-old temple vase with, among other materials, conifer branches and moss-covered branches from the garden.

Preceding spread: A swirling wave of thick green bamboo on the outside of the imperial quarters symbolizes the turbulence of the journey of human life.

Left: A wave of split evergreen bamboo bound with wire in Japanese tradition evokes Kōbō Daishi, or Kūkai, and his journey by ship from China to Japan.

Above: Conical yard-high sculptures feature yellow cornus with white *Oncidium* and *Phalaenopsis* orchids.

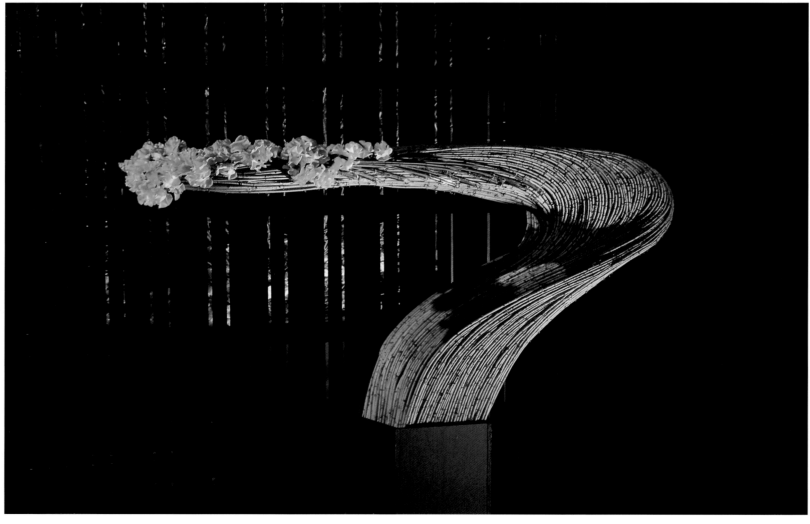

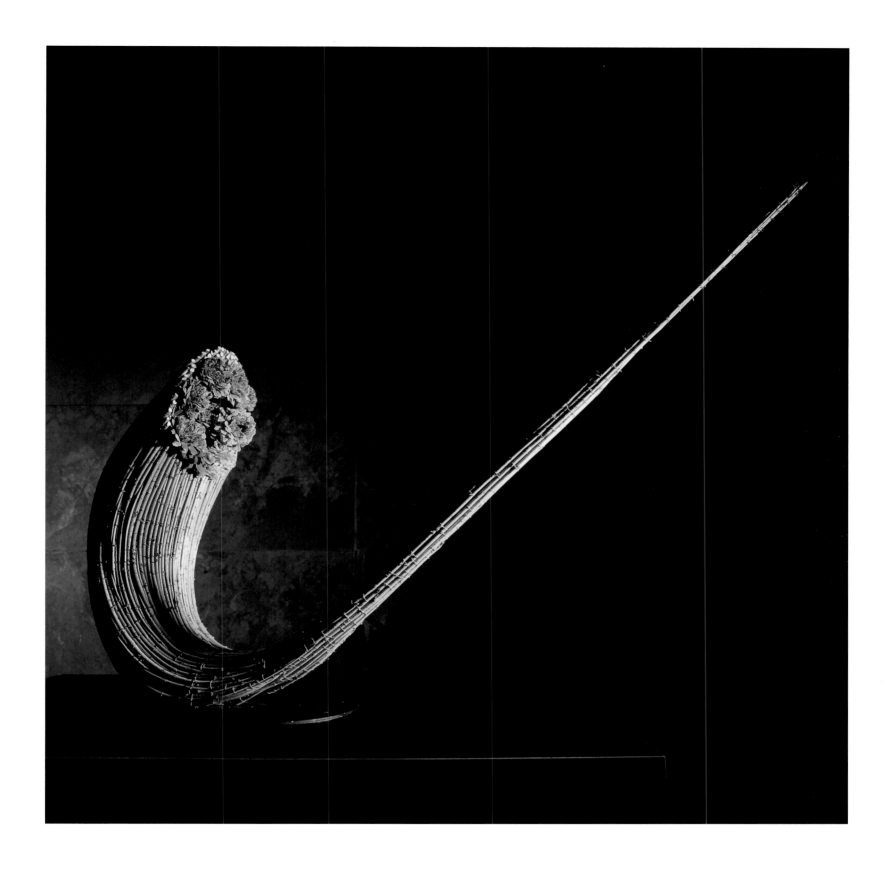

Three sculptures test the technical possibilities of the cornus: above left, black *Cymbidium* orchids; below left, the green sweet pea *Lathyrus* 'Olive Green'; and above, green Japanese buttercups.

Preceding pages: In the old imperial residence, these circular sculptures of brown spindle, *Euonymus alatus*, and green horsetail, *Equisetum hyemale*, with a single white tree peony symbolize winter and spring in Kurashiki.

Left: Spindle and *Lachenalia* flowers form a unique shrine.

Above: This sand, spindle, and sweet pea sculpture in the Buddha room symbolizes the road to the gods, the path to enlightenment.

Following pages: This human-size sculpture echoes the decorative motifs in the temple. The floral foam was cut by laser, then filled with moss and multicolored porcelain berries.

Above and right: A room-size installation
made of the bark of Japanese cedar,
Cryptomeria japonica, and *Oncidium* orchids
refers to the ocean's breaking waves, an
allusion to Kōbō Daishi's, or Kūkai's, arrival by
sea and the founding of Shingon Buddhism.

A composition of needles from the longleaf
pine and sweet peas was inspired by the
silhouette of a table by the Belgian designer
Bernard Duthoy.

An old Japanese ceramic vase from
Yoo Akiyama from the Shinto temple
is ornamented with the black flowers
of hellebore and *Fritillaria camschatcensis.*

CELEBRATIONS & EVENTS

UNFORGETTABLE FLORAL FANTASIES

A noteworthy chapter in the work of Daniel Ost is his floral decor and set designs for wedding celebrations, inaugurations, receptions, memorial services, and festivals. These events frequently involve the ornamentation of entire buildings with the most luxurious, refined, unforgettable fantasies. The designer creates an extravaganza for the senses. Ost can enchant viewers through subtlety, timeless elegance, and fragile beauty, or profoundly impress with grandiose tableaux, utter abundance, and overpowering colors.

This chapter features some of his creations for special events. They are consistently astounding, for example, the canopy of thousands of white orchids for the "40/60 celebrations" of King Baudouin of Belgium in 1990 (referring to the fortieth anniversary of the king's accession to the throne and his sixtieth birthday); the spectacular installation with Ghent azaleas on the roof of the Belgian consulate general on Victoria Peak in Hong Kong; the floating carpet of roses and yards-high rose pillars for the opening of the Museum of Islamic Art in Doha, Qatar; and the sublime wall of flowers composed of thousands of dahlias, gerberas, and other summer flowers in all shades of pink for the fashion show of Dries Van Noten in Paris.

This chapter also features lavish photographs of the annual gala dinner of the Erasmus Foundation for Medical Research at the Université Libre de Bruxelles in the castle of La Hulpe, for which Ost created the floral decorations for many years, featuring, on various occasions, a canopy with moth orchids, chandeliers and garlands made with thousands of strawberries, or a floral evocation of the Silk Road. It includes as well his opulent interior decorations for the exclusive Tsunamachi Mitsui Club in Tokyo and the festive opening of the Palazzo Grassi in Venice, where Ost transformed a hall of the Arsenale into a surrealist tableau with floating figures inspired by René Magritte's painting *Golconda*.

Ost has contributed magical flower creations to numerous wedding ceremonies over the years. For Prince Laurent and Princess Claire of Belgium, he decorated the Brussels Cathedral of St. Michael and St. Gudula with thousands of white azaleas. He has made floral tableaux for princely weddings in Riyadh and Abu Dhabi, and for nonroyal weddings from Puglia, Italy, to Vaux-le-Vicomte, France.

Some of these installations for special events straddle the boundary between floral decoration and garden architecture, for instance, the stylized dike landscape on the Grand Place in Bruges created to commemorate the long tradition of cultivation of the Bruges laurel, or the installation with bromeliad flowers, in the colors of Belgium, for a flower exhibition in the Royal Park Rajapruek in Chiang Mai, Thailand.

In contrast to exhibitions, in which he enjoys a great deal of artistic freedom, for these special occasions Ost must take into account the personality, culture, and specific desires of his client, as well as the selected location, the nature of the event, and of course the climate and the seasons. In no way does this curb his creativity, however, and even less so his craftsmanship. In fact, such events often demand the utmost of the flower designer at a creative, technical, logistical, and even physical level.

Left: A six-yard-high column of floral foam with gypsophila and decorative asparagus, made for a Jewish wedding in Brussels, forms a beacon of light in the dusk.

Preceding spread: Like the nebula of the Milky Way, thousands of *Vanda* orchids in glass tubes hanging on colored sticks float overhead at the annual gala dinner of the Erasmus Foundation in La Hulpe, Belgium.

When he receives a new commission, Ost generally works out his ideas via sketches and impressions in watercolor. Everything is drawn in extraordinary detail, then meticulously planned and prepared. Even so, things can go wrong. Perhaps the flowers he had in mind are not available or cannot be delivered in time or in sufficient quantities. Or perhaps, because they are living things, they are not responding as their handler anticipated. Or they blossom too early or too late, because it is too warm or too cold. Or a sandstorm or a heavy shower upsets the best-laid plans.

Because Ost works with extremely perishable materials—a cut flower is a dying flower—a commission is often a physically and mentally exhausting race against time in order to present what might be thousands of flowers perfectly and in optimal condition. "The type of flower arrangement I practice is a high-level endurance sport," he says. And indeed, this is not the work of a single man, but of a multicultural team of permanent associates as well as dozens—sometimes hundreds—of additional people who, under the all-seeing eye of a demanding master, stay busy day and night helping him realize his floral dreams. For a princely wedding in Abu Dhabi, for instance, more than three hundred individuals worked for days on enormous constructions of hundreds of thousands of white roses and peonies, callas and gypsophilas, which had to be shipped in from around the world. The swaying trees in the Arsenale in Venice were prepared in cold rooms by more than 150 associates in Belgium and then sent to Venice in refrigerated boats. For the wedding of Prince Philippe, more than seventeen tons of flowers were suspended from the centuries-old arches of the cathedral. The thousands of *Vanda* orchids and bromelias necessary for the floral fireworks display at the techno festival Tomorrowland in 2015 had to be watered daily to remain fresh for two weekends.

Ost's floral artworks may not enjoy a long life, it is true, but thanks to the photographs of his creations, their transience can fortunately be overcome. Destined to disappear from the moment that he dreams them up, they are granted eternal life in the pages of this book.

In 2008 this exotic installation with bromeliad flowers in Royal Park Rajapruek in Chiang Mai, Thailand, earned Ost first prize in a flower show.

CELEBRATIONS
OF KING BAUDOUIN
BRUSSELS

On the occasion of the sixtieth birthday of King Baudouin of Belgium, which was also the fortieth anniversary of his accession to the throne, a national tribute was organized. The festivities took place between September 7, 1990 (the king's birthday), and July 21, 1991 (Belgian National Day). For the tribute in the Heysel Palace in Brussels, Ost created an enormous floral canopy of orchids. The designer, still early in his career, spent a month sleeping next to his creation to ensure that nothing would go wrong.

Left and above: The royal floral canopy was covered in fine maidenhair, *Adiantum raddianum*, and ornamented with nine thousand white *Phalaenopsis* orchids.

BELGIAN CONSULATE
HONG KONG

In 1995 the Belgian Consulate in Hong Kong invited Ost to create a grandiose flower spectacle in a unique setting: the tropical gardens of the Belgian consul general's residence on Victoria Peak. The intent was to create a tribute to and a commercial promotion for the Ghent azalea, one of the most important floriculture products of Flanders. Instead of the rare azaleas that were offered to him, Ost chose to use ordinary white and pink Satzuki azaleas in an entirely new manner, to prove that the use of a flower, not its novelty, is what makes it beautiful.

Left and above: A spectacular window made of Ghent azaleas on the roof of the Belgian consul general's residence frames the Hong Kong skyline.

CONRAD HOTEL OPENING
TOKYO

Ost created the flower decorations for the opening of the new Conrad Hotel in Tokyo in 2005. Since then he has often attended to the floral design of the hotel's restaurants. The Conrad Hotel is one of the most luxurious hotels in Tokyo, featuring modern design with a Japanese sensibility. It offers expansive views of Tokyo Bay and the Hamarikyu Gardens.

Left and above: For the main reception room, Ost designed a web of centuries-old bamboo disks and *Gloriosa* lilies. Upon their arrival, guests were welcomed by assistants in traditional Japanese dress carrying the heavy installation.

Above: A sculpture of bamboo, woven kiwi branches, and chestnut shells rests in the hotel lobby.

Right: A human-size installation of citrus peel running from green to yellow occupies a glass vase by L'Anverre.

DRIES VAN NOTEN
FASHION SHOW
PARIS

In 2006 Ost decorated the catwalk for the Paris summer show of the famous Belgian fashion designer Dries Van Noten. Today countless fashion designers work with flower arrangers, but this was the first time a floral artist created such a large-scale installation for a fashion show. Ost remembers the collaboration as intense and challenging: searching for the right colors and flowers, the optimal controlled lines. Van Noten himself is an ardent gardener.

Left and above: Thousands of dahlias, gerberas, *Eustoma*, hydrangeas, and other summer flowers, all in varying shades of pink, form a densely packed backdrop to the runway.

ROYAL WEDDING SHOW
IMPERIAL HOTEL
TOKYO

Ost collaborated with the Japanese cosmetics company Shiseido in 2008 for a Royal Wedding Show in Tokyo's prestigious Imperial Hotel. In addition to festive table and interior decorations, he presented elegant bridal bouquets and sprays for the fashion show. Some were exuberant and lavish, while others evoked Zen-like simplicity.

Left: A model carries an impressive wedding bouquet of steel grass and hyacinths bound with wire.

Above: On the catwalk, a bamboo wreath of entwined calla flowers symbolizes a wedding ring.

LAUREL ON THE MARKET
BRUGES, BELGIUM

In September 2010, on the occasion of the city festival Brugge Centraal, the Bruges market was transformed, in collaboration with the municipal parks department, into a giant laurel garden–to spotlight one of the city's most important export products. Since the nineteenth century, Bruges has enjoyed a flourishing trade in laurels, even supplying the evergreen to imperial Russian families. The laurels from the collection of the Lauretum in Jabbeke, some more than a hundred years old, found a special place in the project. The dike landscape surrounding the Damme Canal near Bruges influenced Ost's design. Besides laurels, he also incorporated the new *Hydrangea paniculata*, nicknamed "Pinky-Winky," into his landscape.

Left, above, and following pages: A stylized dike landscape with laurel trees features hills shaped using laser equipment so that their measurements conform to the plan down to the last centimeter.

TSUNAMACHI MITSUI CLUB
TOKYO

Ost has exhibited his work three times at the distinguished Tsunamachi Mitsui Club in Tokyo. In 1913 the wealthy Mitsui family commissioned the British architect Josiah Conder to design and build the now-historic hotel in which the club is housed. Conder worked as a government advisor during the Meiji period and is considered one of the fathers of modern Japanese architecture.

Left: A fruit mosaic based on a baroque French garden flower bed features elegant garlands of juniper berries.

Above: Rose pillars serve as table decoration.

Above and right: The exuberant floral decoration with garden roses suits the neobaroque architecture of the building.

Above and right: Table decorations feature
pillars and festoons of *Buxus*, as well as white
and pink garden roses. The little crowns on the
rose pillars echo the decoration of the building.

BELFORT
BRUGES, BELGIUM

In 2012, on the occasion of the centenary of the municipal parks department, Ost designed a gigantic "Bouquet for Bruges" in the city's historic Belfort. The belfry is part of a thirteenth-century complex of halls that, in the Middle Ages, served as a storage facility and market. This impressive building is nearly three hundred feet high and consists of two square brick sections topped by an octagonal lantern tower. In 1999 it was made a recognized UNESCO World Heritage Site. Both the upper halls of the Belfort and the inner court were dressed with beautiful floral creations and hundreds of laurels, in a variety of forms.

Left: A floating carpet of flowers measuring sixty by twenty feet planted with eleven thousand verbenas is surrounded by old laurel plants on the inner courtyard of the medieval belfry.

Above: A gateway of bound willow branches leads to a wall of 1,200 red verbenas. A bouquet of 250 *Anthurium* flowers fills the large vase.

ERASMUS FOUNDATION
BRUSSELS

For twenty-five years, Ost designed the floral decorations for the annual gala dinner of the Erasmus Foundation for Medical Research at the Université Libre de Bruxelles, in the castle of La Hulpe near Brussels. Based on French castle architecture, La Hulpe was built in 1840 by the Marquis of Béthune. In the late nineteenth century, the castle (on land that is now part of the Walloon Region) passed into the hands of Ernest Solvay, a chemist and industrialist. It lies on the border of the Sonian Forest in a beautiful park of more than five hundred acres.

Left: This floral firework display required thousands of scarlet plumes, or *Euphorbia fulgens*.

Above: A ceiling installation features thousands of gerberas in different colors.

Capturing the spirit of the Silk Road for
the annual gala dinner of the Erasmus
Foundation, cotton cloths are stretched on
branches and processed with pigments and
sand, then decorated with exotic flowers such
as bougainvillea, begonias, *Vanda* orchids,
fuchsias, and Sahara roses.

Above: A sparkling starry sky is made with thousands of *Phalaenopsis* orchids in glass tubes on a frame of willow branches.

Following pages: This several-yard-long wave made of thousands of sweet peas consumed an entire week's production of the plant from both Belgium and the Netherlands.

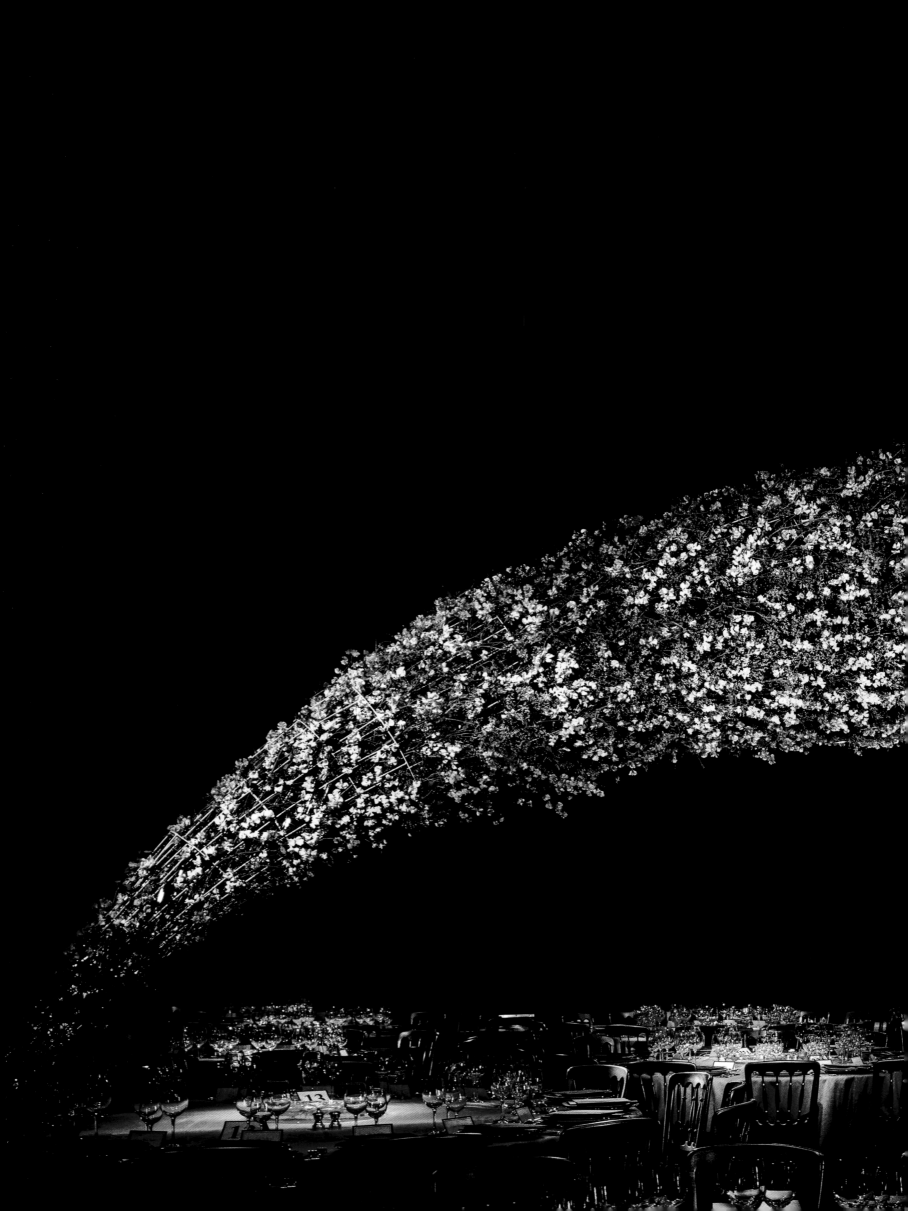

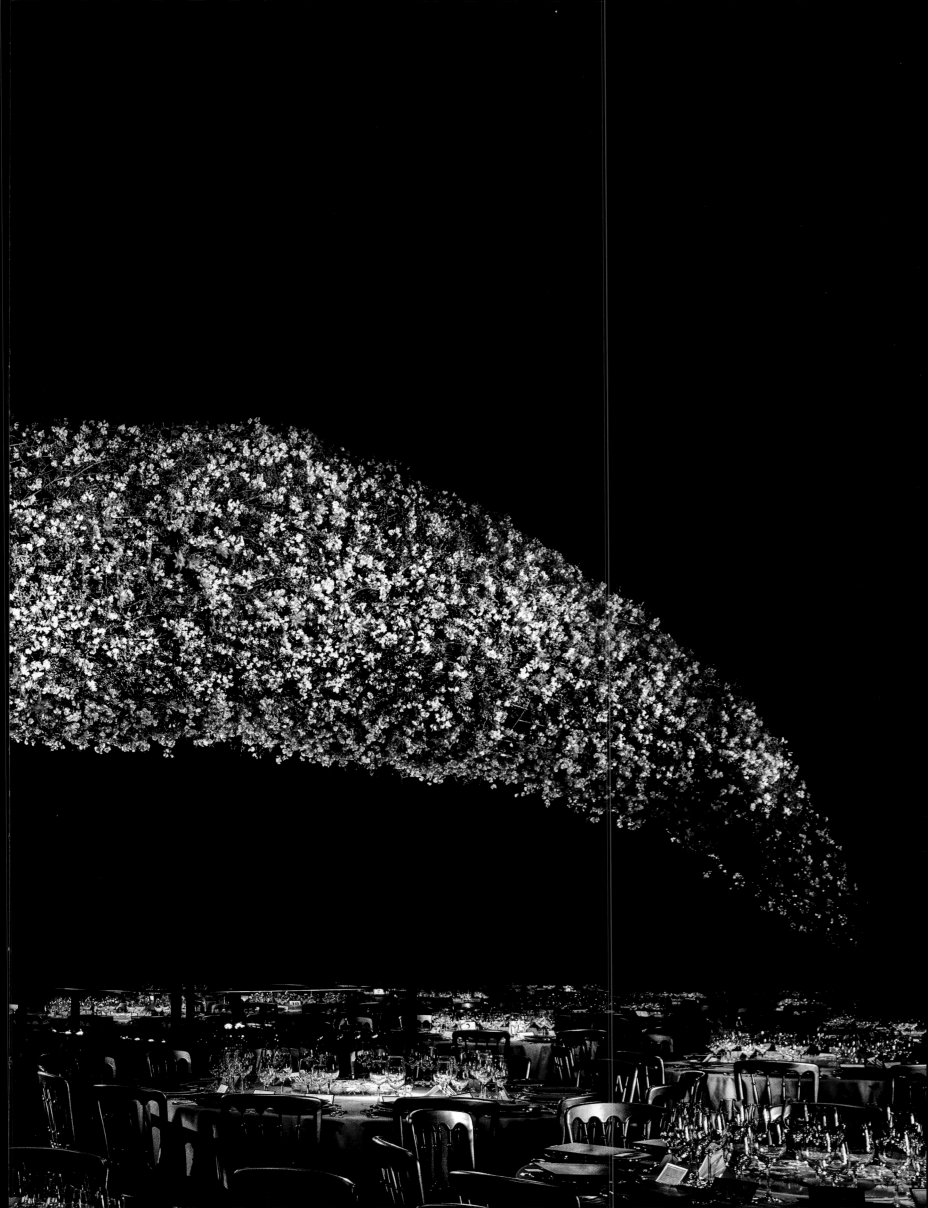

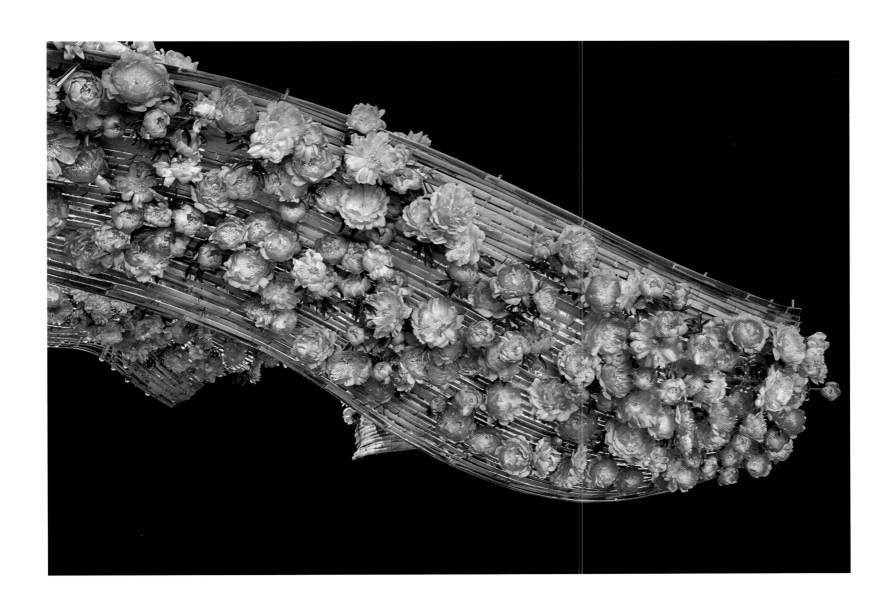

Left: A festive decoration for the tenth anniversary of the Erasmus Foundation features chandeliers and garlands with thousands of strawberries in a weave of olive branches and barley.

Above: Swirling carpets of split bamboo are decorated with rare 'Coral Charm' peonies.

MUSEUM OF ISLAMIC ART OPENING
DOHA

The Museum of Islamic Art in Doha, the capital of Qatar, is built on an artificial peninsula off the Doha Corniche on the Persian Gulf. It was designed by the revered Chinese-American architect I. M. Pei, who looked to ancient Islamic architecture, in particular the celebrated Mosque of Ibn Tulun in Cairo, when designing the museum. A spacious atrium links the structure's multiple buildings, and the large park that surrounds the architectural complex is intended to evoke an Islamic paradise garden. The museum's expansive collection of Islamic art—one of the world's largest—combines work from three different continents and spans a period of some 1,400 years. It includes manuscripts, textiles, ceramics, glass, metalwork, and more. Ost designed the floral scenography for the opening ceremony in November 2008.

Left: The main canal leading to the museum was filled with thousands of rose petals, a reference to the perfumes and colors of the Middle East.

Above: A festoon of cornus is reminiscent of Arabic calligraphy.

Above: Dancing figures of split bamboo counterbalance the measured architecture of I. M. Pei.

Right: Ost surrounded the museum with large pillars of rose petals and chrysanthemums.

ARSENALE
VENICE

On the occasion of the opening of Palazzo Grassi–French industrialist Francois Pinault's art exhibition space in Venice–Ost provided the floral decorations for the banquet held in the Arsenale. The historic Arsenale of Venice was once a complex of shipyards and arms and munitions depots, the oldest buildings of which probably date to 1104. Until the fall of the republic in 1797 at the hands of Napoleon, the Arsenale produced the maritime and merchant vessels that ensured the city's power and wealth. Since 1980 a major part of the imposing industrial complex has been used as an exhibition space for the Venice Biennale.

Left and above: At the inaugural banquet of the Palazzo Grassi, large cypresses of gypsophila hang low above the tables. The enchanting installation pays homage to the floating figures of *Golconda* (1953), a famous painting by the Belgian surrealist René Magritte.

WEDDINGS
VARIOUS LOCATIONS

Ost has designed floral creations for countless weddings around the globe. The events have been held at highly exclusive and spectacular locations, as well as more intimate settings. Like a stage designer, Ost seeks to add luster to these special moments in the lives of the couples and their families, carefully considering their personalities, cultures, and wishes, as well as the locations they choose. Such events often demand the utmost of the flower designer—creatively, technically, logistically, and even physically.

Left and above: The floral decoration for
a wedding in Bangkok includes thousands
of *Dendrobium* and *Phalaenopsis* orchids,
each placed in its own glass test tube.

Above: Laurel is in full regalia for a festive celebration in the Lauretum in Jabbeke, Belgium, a center for laurel cultivation.

Right: Ceiling decorations feature leaves of the South African bird of paradise, *Strelitzia reginae*, hung on nylon threads.

Left and above: More than three hundred people worked for days to create this vast installation with hundreds of thousands of white roses and peonies, callas, and gypsophila for a princely wedding in Abu Dhabi.

For the wedding of Prince Laurent and
Princess Claire of Belgium in 2003, Ost
decorated the Brussels Cathedral of St.
Michael and St. Gudula with thousands
of white azaleas, the pride of Ghent
floriculture.

In December 1999, Ost dressed up the
Cathedral of St. Michael and St. Gudula
for the wedding of Crown Prince Philippe
and Princess Mathilde of Belgium.
Thousands of white and pink cut flowers,
weighing more than seventeen tons
in total, hung in the air on long cables.

Above: White hortensias and various garden-picked branches hang from the ceiling in large Plexiglas dishes.

Below: This wedding on a horse farm in Belgium featured discreet table decorations consisting of white twigs with approximately twenty types of white flowers, including sweet peas, roses, and *Eustoma*. Note the horse looking on from the stall in the back.

Above: Table decorations of bamboo and Japanese *Dendrobium* orchids evoke champagne bottles being uncorked.

Below: Table and ceiling decorations feature white *Vanda* orchids.

Rose garlands welcome the bridal
couple at the Château de Vaux-le-
Vicomte in Maincy, France.

Distinguished garlands of *Buxus* leaves
decorated with lemon and white spray roses
hang overhead in this festive wedding tent.

Above: The decoration for this wedding in France reflects the sensibility of the luxurious tent. The horseshoe-shaped constructions are ornamented with roses and white spring flowers, such as nigella, campanula, great masterwort, columbine, and bleeding hearts.

Right: A beguiling setting for a royal wedding in Abu Dhabi features a stage construction decorated with Japanese peonies for which Ost used the old *faux bois*, or rustic cement, technique.

Above, right, and following pages:
For an opulent wedding in the desert
climate of Riyadh, Saudi Arabia, Ost
designed giant pillars and sunshades
with colorful *Kalanchoe*.

Above and right: For a dreamlike Indian
wedding in the Italian region of Puglia,
Ost conceived gossamer-thin sunshades
with *Vanda* orchids and bougainvillea
suspended from brightly colored sticks.

Left: White roses offer an elegant welcome to a young bridal couple.

Above: A flower carpet on the Grote Markt of Sint-Niklaas featuring begonias and small cobbles is intended to evoke the windows of the neo-Gothic town hall.

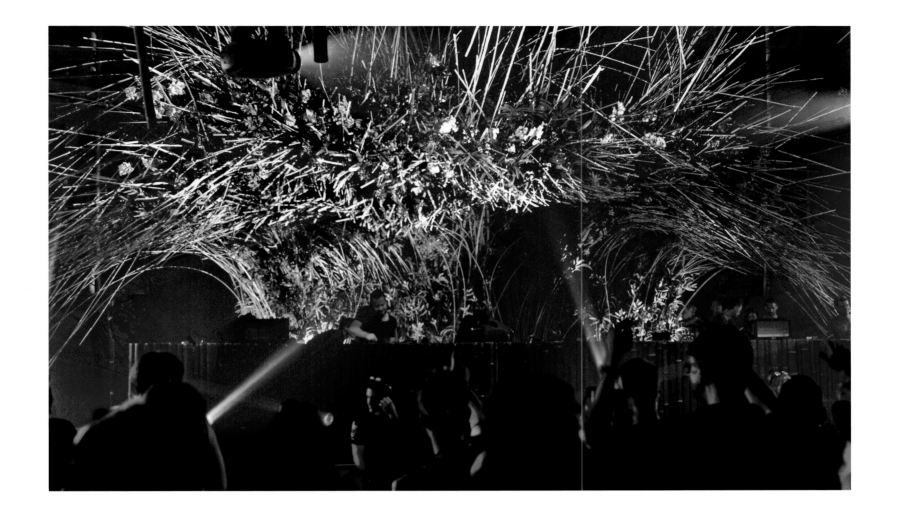

TOMORROWLAND
MUSIC FESTIVAL
ANTWERP

Tomorrowland is an outdoor dance festival that takes place in De Schorre Park near Antwerp, Belgium. Launched in 2005, it has grown into the world's biggest techno festival, drawing hundreds of thousands of visitors from around the globe, and has expanded to include festivals in Atlanta and São Paulo. For the 2014 jubilee edition, Ost designed spectacular floral decoration for the Garden of Madness, a temporary building that drifts on pontoons in a pond.

Left and above: A floral firework in the Garden of Madness featured thousands of *Vanda* orchids and bromelias, which were watered daily from an elevated platform.

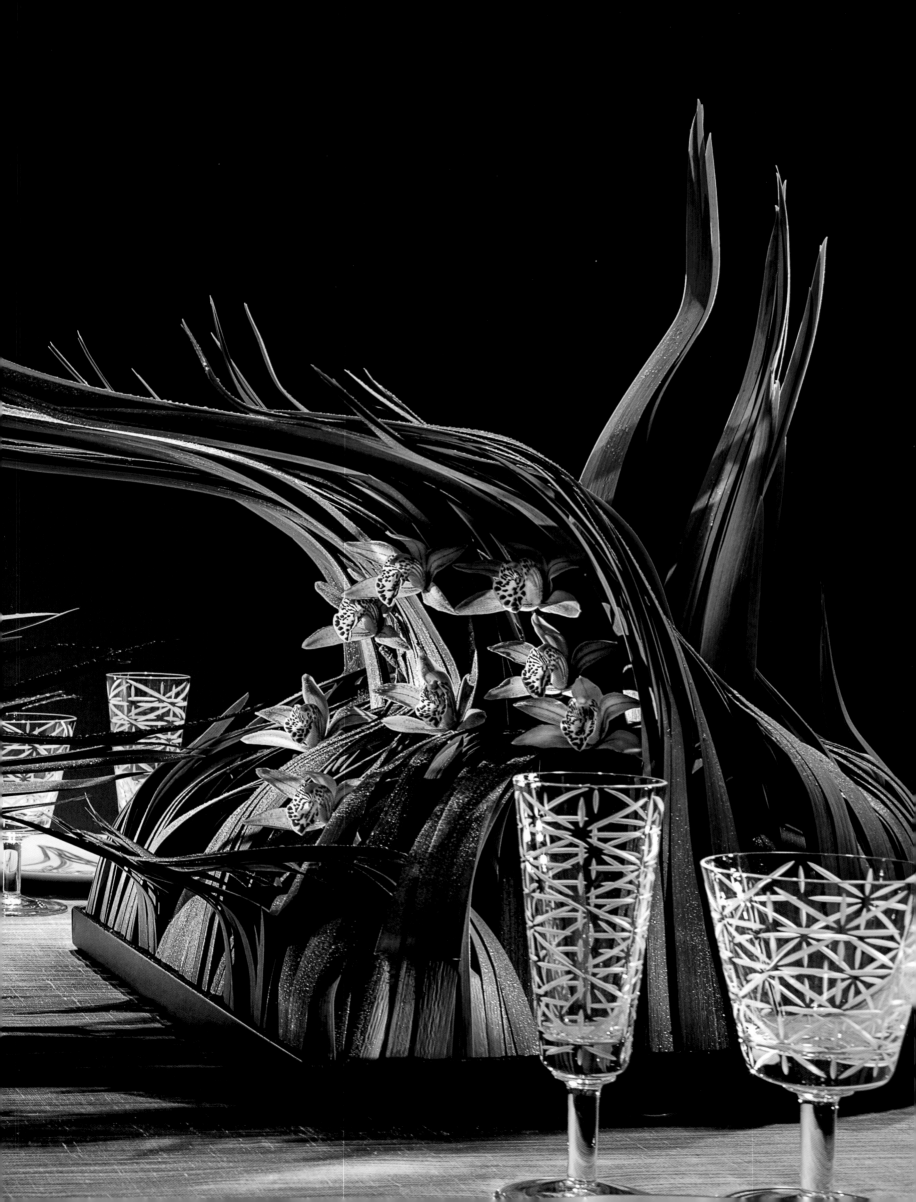

ATMOSPHERE & DECORATIONS

SEEING BEAUTY IN THE EPHEMERAL

One puts you into a simple vase–
everything changes;
it may be the same phrase,
but sung by an angel.

–Rainer Maria Rilke, *The Roses*

This chapter presents a number of flower pieces, interior decorations, and table decorations that illustrate the more intimate, domestic aspect of Daniel Ost's floral work. What is immediately strik-ing about these creations is his particular sensitivity to the forms, colors, and structures of the flowers and plants, as well as the particular vessels that contain them. The objective is always an exquisite balance between plant and vase. When looking at many of these pieces, the philosophical question inevitably arises as to whether the form and color of the vase dictated Ost's choice of natural materials, or whether the vase only came into its full existence by the grace of the flowers, leaves, and branches that Ost chose for that arrangement. This holds true for his "classical" bou-quets, such as those for the visit of Prince Philippe and Princess Mathilde to Japan, as well as for the more abstract compositions, such as the leaf sculptures he designed for the vases of B&B Italia.

Even very simple glass vases, when treated or wrapped, can take on a unique character. Whether made of crystal, porcelain, wood, bronze, or silver, the vases are often rare and one-of-a-kind. Some are centuries-old collection pieces. Others are the work of renowned contemporary designers, such as Bořek Šípek, Ken Matsuzaki, Shiro Tsujimura, David Huycke, and the Belgian glass artists group L'Anverre. Ost has collaborated over the years with numerous ceramicists, glass artists, woodworkers, and other craftspeople and designers to create special objects to hold his work.

For his table decorations, as in all of his work, Ost strives for a symbiosis in form, color, and atmosphere, in this case among the floral creations, the table service, the linen, and the surround-ing space. He always tries to integrate the season, as well. Fine examples include the hunting table with deer antlers and mushrooms, which alludes to the dinner service and the motif in the china, and the summer table with summer flowers, which echoes the flowers in the Flora Danica dinner service by Royal Copenhagen.

What also stands out as one leafs through this book is how Ost continuously balances between two worlds: Flemish abundance and excess on the one hand, and sober Japanese sim-plicity and abstraction on the other. Over the years he has become increasingly influenced by Japanese flower arranging and profoundly moved by the culture's reverence for flowers and plants. "In Japan," he says, "I learned how to work with the soul of the flowers, to observe the uniqueness of each flower, not just the form and the color. Also to grasp the symbolic significance of flowers and how one can use flowers to create an atmosphere in a space. To see beauty in what

Left: Twenty people worked for seven days on this lush Christmas table at the Imperial Hotel in Tokyo. The garlands and festoons with *Buxus* leaves and roses reference the neo-Gothic wedding hall in Ost's native city of Sint-Niklaas.

Preceding spread: A table decoration features sculpted iris leaves and Japanese orchids.

is incomplete and ephemeral, in what is weathered or consumed. That is *wabi-sabi*, the awareness that beauty often rests in the details and manifests itself in incompleteness. It is also about what to leave out and what is the essence. For the Japanese, complexity often implies immaturity or decadence, whereas simplicity is never simple."

On the other hand, Ost has little affinity with traditional Japanese flower arranging. As he explains:

> That is all codified; it keeps repeating itself and hardly allows for any creativity. What I'm trying to do is to approach Western floral arrangement with a Japanese mentality. The Japanese recognize in my work a number of elements that are very important to them, for instance, clear lines, a certain way of using color, my choice of materials, the foundations with which I work, my preference for art nouveau. For them, with their ikebana tradition, I am a kind of bridge between East and West. But I am and remain a child of the land of Velvet Brueghel, with those magnificent classical bouquets. Even though lavish arrangements appeal less to me from a creative perspective in recent years—the older I get, the more I want to leave out, to reach the pure essence, to say more with less—I certainly don't look down on them. On the contrary. That is an art in itself, especially if, like myself, you are a perfectionist.

When Ost makes a Burgundian bouquet, the challenge lies especially in the choice of materials and the precise color scheme: "The floral still lifes from the Golden Age do not show real flower pieces. Their makers did not master the technique of actually bringing together such botanic diversity, nor did they work with flowers from different seasons," he says. "They are fantasies. Whereas now we have the possibility to make any combination whatsoever, using flowers flown in from any corner of the world. The challenge today is therefore also to make something with real flowers and plants that is at least as good as, or even better than, what our predecessors imagined."

This composition with magnolia leaf and yellow
berries echoes the colors of the painting behind
it at the school of Laethem-Saint-Martin in the
Salons for Fine Arts in Sint-Niklaas. The glassware
is from the collection of the former Shah of Iran.

IMPERIAL HOTEL
TOKYO

Ost once again participated in the Christmas exhibition at the distinguished Imperial Hotel, in collaboration with Shiseido and Lexus. Although the hotel was founded in 1890, the current structure dates to the 1970s and replaces an iconic building from the 1920s designed by the American architect Frank Lloyd Wright (a few mementos remain in the elegant art deco Old Imperial Bar).

Left: A winter-inspired scene of bent cornus with apples welcomes visitors.

Above: White orchids on bamboo sticks resemble flickering fireworks

Above: A scene with white spring flowers on trays is suspended on birch branches.

Right: A massive bamboo sculpture incorporates poinsettias, moss, and rice grains.

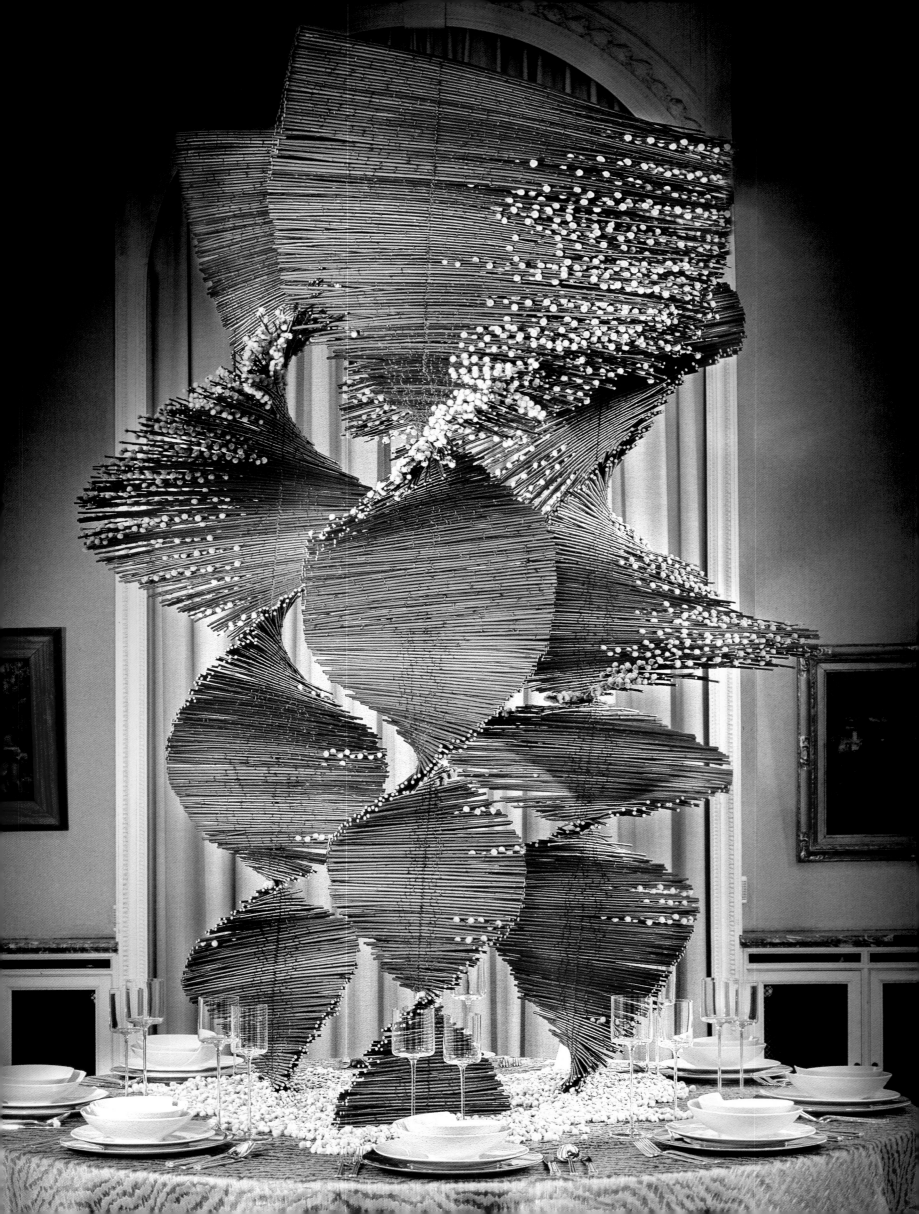

DANIEL OST AT HOME
SINT-NIKLAAS

In 2008 Ost presented his work in his hometown of Sint-Niklaas at the exhibition *Daniel Ost at Home* in the luxurious Salons of Fine Arts, a monumental town house with a remarkable art collection. Designed by the Antwerp architect Paul Stordiau, it was built in 1928 for the textile manufacturer Edmond Meert. With a majestic staircase, richly ornamented marble mantelpieces, and stuccoed ceilings, it possesses the grandeur of an eighteenth-century French castle. For this exhibition, the company Home-Interior from Lokeren commissioned Flemish weavers to craft the tablecloth, and the De Wolf company from Sint-Niklaas provided the utensils and exceptional dining service.

Left: Waves of willow catkins serve as table decoration.

Above: A hunting-themed table features deer antlers with branches, mushrooms, and moss. The dining service is decorated with mushrooms, and the cutlery is made of deer antlers.

TAKASHIMAYA
TOKYO

Takashimaya is a luxury department store originally founded as a used clothing shop in Kyoto in the early nineteenth century, at the end of the Edo period. The store now has locations in the major Japanese cities, as well as in China, Singapore, and Paris. The shop in the Nihonbashi part of Tokyo dates to 1933 and was designed by Sadataro Takahashi, then a leading Japanese architect. The building is famous for its unique Shōwa architecture and design, a subtle blend of historical Western and Japanese influences, and is widely valued for its cultural heritage. Ost was invited here in 2009 for an exhibition of table decorations.

Left and above: An exuberant spring tableau features dozens of flowers that echo the Flora Danica dining service by Royal Copenhagen. The flowers are set in glass tubes sewn into the cloth.

Above: A champagne table is adorned with the white flowers of *Ixia*.

Below: Table decorations with iris leaves and Japanese orchids poetically respond to the motif in the tableware.

Below: An airy table decoration utilizes Japanese tree peonies.

Above: A table decoration based on willow branches incorporates *Eustoma,* sweet peas, roses, and fern.

Following pages: Left, green bamboo and snake allium come together in a bold decoration. Right, a table decoration features steel grass and lilies of the valley above, and summer snowflakes, or *Leucojum aestivum,* below.

Above: A cornucopia of steel grass is combined with Japanese *Clematis montana*.

Right: A composition of steel grass is decorated with the white leaf tips of *Aspidistra elatior* 'Asahi,' cut into small squares.

Following pages: An iconic flower table of Plexiglas is adorned with dozens of types of summer flowers floating in water.

CHRISTMAS DECORATION TOWN HALL
SINT-NIKLAAS

In 2010 the historic town hall of Sint-Niklaas became the setting for *Daniel Ost: Christmas Days*.
Twenty-five Japanese interns traveled to Belgium to help prepare the exhibition. The entire town
hall was bathed in a sea of flowers, including countless new varieties of orchids and bromelias,
and a number of exceptional new roses from the specialized rose nursery Wim Van Kampen in
the Netherlands. One of these was the Ivanhoe, a warm-red rose with a green heart. In addition,
Ost was given exclusive authorization from the Agency for Nature and Forest to pick plants and
branches from a number of parks and nature reserves.

Left: An expansive construction of green and
red lacquered bamboo in the entrance hall
and stairwell responds to the architecture
of the neo-Gothic building.

Above: The forms and colors of this lavish
table setting reflect the town hall's neo-
Gothic architecture and decor. The garlands
on the mantelpiece are made of red roses
and the berries of *Ilex verticillata*.

A playful table decoration features
needles and bark from the black pine.

This table decoration is inspired by the colors
and forms of the tableware, and is composed
of the leaf of white poplar and the berries
of *Ilex verticillata*.

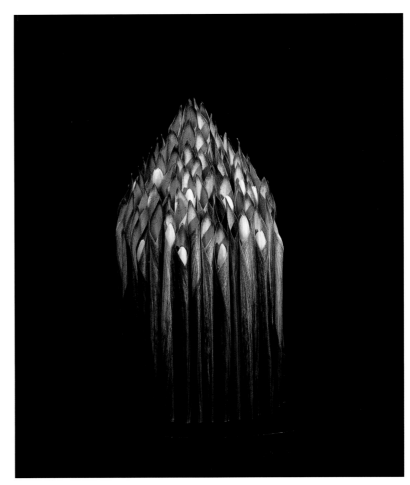

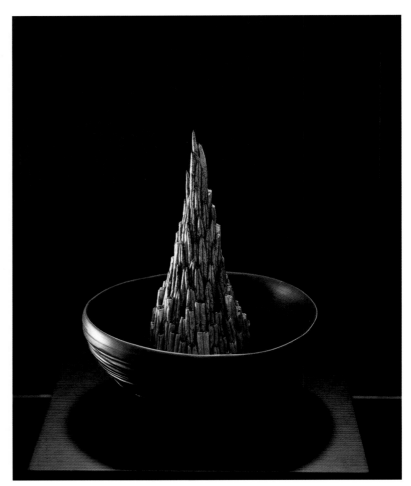

B&B ITALIA
TOKYO

An invitation from the Japanese branch of the Italian design company B&B Italia to participate in an exhibition in Tokyo was an ideal opportunity for Ost to experiment with soberly designed contemporary glass and ceramic objects. Using simple means, Ost pursued the essence of a design and its relationship to the vessel. Here we see several fine examples of his achievement: although these abstract arrangements may seem simple, they were challenging to execute.

Left: These minimalist but technically demanding compositions using the leaf of the lotus and the leaf of *Aspidistra elatior* 'Asahi' (top right) pair well with the vases of B&B Italia.

Above: A fanciful imitation of a natural form uses the colorful leaf of *Aspidistra elatior* 'Asahi.'

BELGIAN EMBASSY
TOKYO

The Belgian royal household maintains close relations with the Imperial House of Japan, a friendship that reaches back generations to the Belgian King Albert I. The ties between Japan and Belgium intensified in 1953, when the then-Crown Prince Akihito and the young King Baudouin met at the coronation of Elizabeth II. In 2012, when Belgian Crown Prince Philippe and Princess Mathilde led a trade mission to Japan, they were received for a private visit at the Imperial Palace in Tokyo. For the official reception at the Belgian embassy in Tokyo, Ost created a number of intimate bouquets that stood out for their refined forms and colors, and the poetic resonance between flower and vase.

Left and above: In these elegant bouquets, the vertical bamboo shoots, large red peonies, and transparent plumes of the smoke tree, *Cotinus coggygria*, play a prominent role.

Above and right: What is special about these bouquets with clouds of the smoke tree, large peony flowers, and very rare Japanese *Eustoma* flowers is that the flowers are not set in floral foam, but are fixed to the edges of the vases with small branches.

SPLENDID TABLE DECORATIONS
MATSUZAKAYA
NAGOYA

Matsuzakaya is the largest department store in Japan, and also one of the oldest in the world. With locations in Europe, Matsuzakaya has always paid close attention to the cultural and economic exchanges between Japan and the West. In 1924 it was the first department store in Japan in which visitors were not expected to take off their shoes. In Nagoya, the store includes a museum where Western art and culture are presented. Ost displayed his work there in 2012 for the exhibition *Splendid Table Decorations*.

Left: The white flowers of *Curcuma* harmonize with the crystal Baccarat vase.

Above: A vegetal table landscape features grapes, melons, and the marbled leaf of *Anthurium crystallinum*.

Above: A spring tableau echoes the colors of the Flora Danica dining service.

Above right: An exotic bouquet incorporates *Bromeliaceae*.
Below right: A delicate bouquet features the flowers of the smoke tree and southern African *Disa* orchid.

Following pages: This five-yard-high installation symbolizes the deadly tsunami of 2011. With this creation Ost hoped to hearten his Japanese students and assistants. The bamboo shoots represent humankind standing up after a natural disaster.

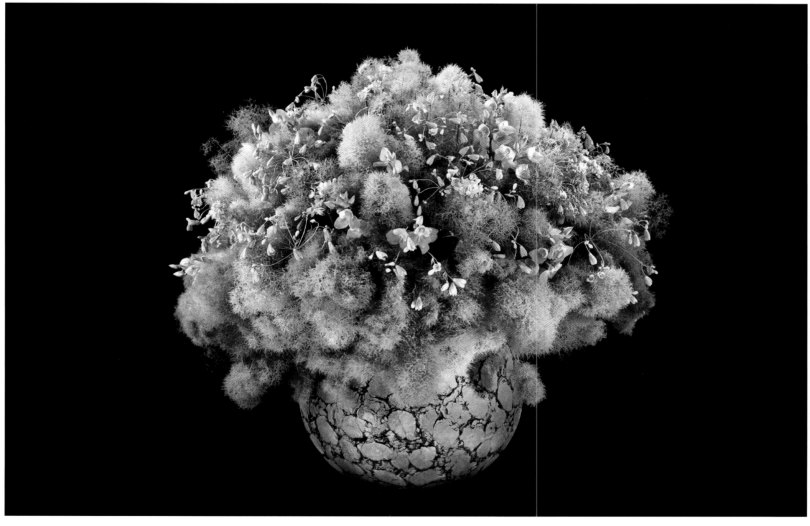

BOTANICAL INFORMATION

2
Ampelopsis brevipedunculata
Ash
Rice grains

4–5
Arisaema sp.
Xanthorrhoea sp.

8
Vanda sp.
Charred wood
Vase by Kosta Boda (Sweden)

10
Rosa 'President Hoover'
Rose thorns
Glass vase

13
Iris germanica 'Beige Butterfly'
Typha latifolia
Bronze vase

14
Cornus sanguinea 'Viridissima'
Italian berries

17
Cornus alba 'Sibirica'

18
Diospyros kaki
Berries of *Rhaphiolepis umbellata*
Berries of *Smilax china*
Ash
Clay

20
Eucalyptus sp.

23
Aspidistra elatior

24
Platycerium grande
Lead
Wood

26
Allium porrum

28
Allium porrum
Clay

29
Cornus sanguinea 'Viridissima'
Cyrtanthus sp.
Lachenalia
Lilium bulbiferum

30
Allium porrum
Clay

31
Pinus maritima
Pinus sylvestris

32–33
Lunaria annua

34
Cornus alba 'Sibirica'
Salix matsudana 'Tortuosa'

35
Brassica oleracea
Cucurbita
Dendrocalamus giganteus

36
Brassica oleracea
Nelumbo nucifera

37
Dischidia pectinoides
Ceramic dish by Lebuin D'Haese
   (Belgium)

38
Salix sp.
Xerophyllum tenax

39
Fruit of *Malus* sp.
Salix alba var. *vitellina*

40–41
Iris ensata
Clay

42
Allium porrum
Hydrangea macrophylla
   Teller Series
Lemna
Viburnum lantana
Charred wood

43
Hydrangea macrophylla cv.
Prunus spinosa
Clay

44
Encephalartos laurentianus
Larix decidua

45
Elaeagnus × ebbingei
Eucalyptus
Cast-iron slab

46
Brunia albiflora

47
Coral
Cornus alba 'Sibirica'

48
Fritillaria persica 'Adiyaman'
Strelitzia reginae

49
Clematis vitalba
Quercus robur

50
Chamaecyparis obtusa 'Filicoides'

51
Juniperus chinensis
   'Aureovariegata'
Taraxacum officinale

52
Papaver nudicaule
Scirpus sp.
Glass pane

53
Soleirolia soleirolii
Ice

54
Hydrangea macrophylla cv.
Sambucus nigra
Xerophyllum tenax
Ceramic vase by Mobach
   (the Netherlands)

55
Narcissus 'Las Vegas'
Plexiglas

56
Rosa 'Florence'
Porcelain vase by Roos
   Van de Velde (Belgium)

57
Nymphaea alba

58
Papaver rhoeas

59
Celosia argentea var. *cristata* cv.
Tussilago farfara

60
Leontopodium alpinum
Tussilago farfara

61
Berries of *Paeonia suffruticosa*
Tussilago farfara

62
Anthurium andraeanum 'Marble'
Typha

63
Arisaema sikokianum
Chaenomeles fruit
Passiflora
Oxidized metal by
   Emiko Nakamura (Japan)

64
Papaver rhoeas

65
Autumn leaves of various
   Prunus sp.

66
Cucurbita

67
Bergenia sp.
Papaver nudicaule
Glass by Kosta Boda (Sweden)

68
Left:
Rosa 'Toscanini'
Chinese bronze vase
   from the Han dynasty
Right:
Petals of various flowers
Rosa cv.

69
Rose petals
Silver vase from Tantansai

70
Above left:
Enkianthus sp.
Paeonia suffruticosa cv.
Antique bronze vase
   from the Han dynasty
Above right:
Eustoma grandiflorum
Pueraria montana
Wrought-iron and glass vase
   by Bořek Šípek (Czech Republic)
Below:
Acanthopanax sessiliflorus
Actaea rubra
Aralia californica
Euonymus americanus
Euonymus hamiltonianus
Gramineae
Magnolia sp.
Nerine sp.
Rubus
Sambucus aralia
Bronze vase by Mobach
   (the Netherlands)

71
Actaea rubra
Anemone hupehensis var. *japonica*
Aralia californica
Decaisnea fargesii
Gramineae
Hydrangea macrophylla cv.
Leycesteria formosa
Malus sp.
Prunus persica cv.
Ceramic vase by Mobach
   (the Netherlands)

72
Ranunculus asiaticus cv.

73
Anomatheca laxa
Cornus alba 'Sibirica'

74
Tetradium daniellii var. *hupehensis*
Zea mays 'Japonica Multicolor'

75
Acer
Malus 'Profusion'
Ribes rubrum
Ulmus
Viburnum odoratissimum
Technical execution by
   Jan Poelmans (Belgium)
   with Elly Lin (Taiwan)
Tea set by Roos Van de Velde
   (Belgium)

76
Impatiens sp.
Musa sp.
Glass vase by Paolo Venini (Italy)

77
Lemna
Zantedeschia sp.
Metal vase

78
Magnolia grandiflora
Ceramic vase by Ken
   Matsuzaki (Japan)

79
Paphiopedilum 'Vintner's Treasure'
Charred *Phyllostachys edulis*

80
Muscari sp.
Silver vase by David Huycke
   (Belgium)

81
Ribes rubrum

82
Narcissus 'Las Vegas'
Pinus palustris

83
Pinus palustris
Rosa 'Pure'

84
Disa uniflora cv.
Pinus palustris

85
Disa uniflora cv.
Charred *Phyllostachys edulis*

86–87
Aesculus hippocastanum
Autumn leaves of *Prunus* sp.

A single flower of the flesh-eating trumpet
pitcher, *Sarracenia*, perches on a structure
of red cornus.

88
Cornus alba 'Sibirica'
Eucalyptus niphophila
Salix sp.

89
Cercidiphyllum sp.
Diospyros sp.
Prunus sp.
Wood and metal frame

90
Chrysanthemum sp.
Phyllostachys edulis
Salix matsudana 'Tortuosa'
Glass vases by L'Anverre (Belgium)

92
Phyllostachys edulis

93
Berries of *Ilex verticillata*

95
Helianthus sp.
Lavandula angustifolia

96
Camellia japonica cv.
Prunus sp.
Ash of *Prunus* sp.
Leaves of *Ternstroemia
   gymnanthera*
Clay

97
Cornus sanguinea 'Viridissima'
Lemna
Prunus sp.
Ash of *Prunus* sp.
Clay
Plexiglas

98-99
Leucobryum glaucum
Paederia scandens var. *mairei*
Sinomenium acutum
Clay

100
Xanthorrhoea sp.

101
Cornus alba 'Sibirica'

102
Above left:
Iris ensata
Vase by Shiro Tsujimura (Japan)

Above right:
Chamaerops humilis
Pterostylis baptistii

Below left:
Xanthorrhoea sp.

Below right:
Typha latifolia

103
Arisaema ringens
Aspidistra elatior
Chamaerops humilis
Paphiopedilum sp.

104
Above:
Xanthorrhoea sp.

Below left:
Ampelopsis brevipedunculata
Cornus alba 'Kesselringii'

Below right:
Pinus palustris

105
Euonymus alatus
Trichosanthes cucumeroides

106
Berries of *Smilax china*

107
Berries of *Smilax china*
Driftwood

108
Above:
Magnolia obovata
Zinc and copper

Below:
Ampelopsis brevipedunculata
Ash of *Prunus* sp.

109
Chrysanthemum sp.
Paper by Eriko Horiki &
   Associates (Japan)

110
Chrysanthemum sp.
Euonymus alatus

111
Above:
Chrysanthemum sp.
Clay
Dried leaves

Below:
Gypsophila 'Million Stars'
Xanthorrhoea sp.

112
Cornus alba 'Sibirica'

113
Pinus thunbergii

114
Salix alba 'Tristis'
Solanum tuberosum

115
Papaver nudicaule
Paper bags

116
Above:
Equisetum hyemale
Eragrostis curvula
Vase by Lee In-Chin
   (South Korea)

Below:
Equisetum hyemale
Petasites japonicus
Phragmites australis

117
Carex conica
Cosmos atrosanguineus
   'Black Beauty'

118
Ranunculus asiaticus cv.
Xanthorrhoea sp.

119
Cornus alba 'Sibirica'
Iris sp.

120
Vanda sp.
Driftwood

121
Cornus sanguinea 'Viridissima'

122
Coccoloba uvifera
Vanda sp.

123
Autumn leaves
Wood

124
Cornus sanguinea 'Viridissima'
Smilax china

125
Cornus alba 'Sibirica'
Gloriosa superba cv.

126-27
Berries of *Smilax china*
Cornus sanguinea 'Viridissima'

128
Cornus alba 'Sibirica'
Hydrangea macrophylla cv.

129
Berries of *Fatsia japonica*
Cornus alba 'Sibirica'
Leucobryum glaucum

130
Aspidistra sp.
Rose petals

131
Cornus sanguinea 'Viridissima'

132
Magnolia grandiflora
Ceramic vase by
   Ken Matsuzaki (Japan)

133
Magnolia grandiflora
Ceramic vase by Ken
   Matsuzaki (Japan)

134
*Ampelopsis brevipedunculata
   variegata*
Wood
Vase by Masakichi Awashima
   (Japan)

135
*Ampelopsis brevipedunculata
   variegata*
Cornus alba
Vase by Masakichi Awashima
   (Japan)

136-37
*Ampelopsis brevipedunculata
   variegata*
Magnolia grandiflora

138
Above:
Ampelopsis brevipedunculata
Floral foam
Slate by Isamu Noguchi
   (Japan / United States)

Below:
Leucobryum glaucum
Ash of *Prunus* sp.
Floral foam

139
Paulownia tomentosa

140-41
Cucurbita
Japanese rope

142
Leaves and flowers of
   Camellia japonica
Ash of *Prunus* sp.
Plexiglas

143
Rhododendron indicum
Prunus sp.
Tulipa sp.

144-45
Cryptomeria japonica
Phyllostachys edulis

146
Cornus alba 'Sibirica'
Fritillaria camschatcensis

147
Cornus alba 'Sibirica'
Fritillaria camschatcensis
Leucobryum glaucum
Phyllostachys edulis

148-49
Cornus alba 'Sibirica'
Leucobryum glaucum
Phyllostachys edulis

150
Phyllostachys edulis

151
Phyllostachys edulis

152
Leucobryum glaucum
Petasites japonicus
Ash of *Prunus* sp.
Clay

153
Leucobryum glaucum

154
Phyllostachys edulis
Stemona japonica

155
Asparagus asparagoides
Clematis sp.
Phyllostachys edulis

156-57
Split *Phyllostachys edulis*

158
Cornus alba 'Sibirica'
Paeonia suffruticosa

159
Above:
Cornus alba 'Sibirica'

Below left:
Pieris japonica 'Katsura'

Below right:
Cornus alba 'Sibirica'

160
Paeonia suffruticosa
Phyllostachys edulis

161
Arisaema sp.
Cornus alba 'Kesselringii'

162
Aspidistra elatior
Euonymus alatus

163
Prunus sp.

164
Above left:
Camellia japonica 'Shiratama'
Euonymus alatus

Above right:
Camellia japonica
Corylus avellana 'Contorta'

Below:
Euonymus alatus
Zantedeschia aethiopica cv.

165
Camellia japonica 'Shiratama'
Leaves of *Prunus* sp.

166
Euonymus alatus
Salix sp.

167
Above:
Symplocarpus foetidus
Ash
Clay

Below:
Euonymus alatus
Eustoma sp.
Salix sp.

168
Cornus alba 'Sibirica'
Passiflora sp.
Ranunculus asiaticus 'Charlotte'

169
Callicarpa
Eustoma grandiflora
   'Marron Brown'
Paulownia tomentosa
Bronze vase by Domani
   (Belgium)

170
Aspidistra elatior

171
Xanthorrhoea sp.
Crystal vase by Baccarat (France)

172
Berries of *Nandina domestica*
Charred *Phyllostachys edulis*

173
Berries of *Ilex verticillata*
Xanthorrhoea sp.

174-75
Cornus alba 'Sibirica'
Hippeastrum sp.

176
Aspidistra elatior
Vases by L'Anverre (Belgium)

177
Clematis sp.
Helianthus sp.
Phyllostachys edulis

178
Leucobryum glaucum
Phyllostachys edulis
Zantedeschia sp.

179
Leaves of Aspidistra elatior
Phyllostachys edulis

180
Cornus alba 'Sibirica'
Xanthorrhoea sp.
Glass vases by L'Anverre (Belgium)

181
Dianthus sp.
Salix sp.
Glass vases by L'Anverre (Belgium)

182
Above:
Cornus alba 'Sibirica'
Berries of Smilax china

Below:
Cornus alba 'Sibirica'

183
Above:
Camptotheca acuminata
Cornus alba 'Sibirica'

Below:
Cornus alba 'Sibirica'

184
Laurus nobilis
Rosa cv.

185
Grass
Rosa cv.

186
Prunus sp.
Metal

187
Iris laevigata
Phyllostachys edulis
Japanese lacquerware container

188-89
Cornus alba 'Sibirica'

190
Camellia quephongensis
Cornus alba 'Sibirica'

191
Split Phyllostachys edulis

192
Iris ensata
Paphiopedilum japonica

193
Xanthorrhoea sp.

194
Clematis spp.
Vase of cut bamboo
   by Nakagawa (Japan)

195
Fritillaria pallidiflora
Leucobryum glaucum
Phyllostachys edulis
Xanthorrhoea sp.
Japanese lacquerware container
Walnut

196
Camellia japonica cv.

197
Split Phyllostachys edulis

198
Branches of Cornus alba
   'Winter Flame'
Zantedeschia 'Dreamy Pink'

199
Cornus alba 'Winter Flame'
Rosa cv.

200
Clematis sp.
Phyllostachys edulis

201
Aspidistra elatior
Leucobryum glaucum
Phyllostachys edulis

202-3
Grass
Leucobryum glaucum
Soleirolia soleirolii
Verbena 'Thalys Cream White'
Japanese rocks

204-5
Prunus sp.
Plexiglas

206
Buxus
Laurus nobilis
Zantedeschia aethiopica

207
Laurus nobilis

208
Above:
Xanthorrhoea sp.
Zantedeschia sp.

Below:
Cornus alba 'Sibirica'
Gloriosa sp.

209
Leucobryum glaucum
Charred Phyllostachys edulis
Metal frame

210
Above left:
Washingtonia filifera
Vase by L'Anverre (Belgium)

Above right:
Aspidistra elatior 'Asahi'
Glass vases by L'Anverre (Belgium)

Below:
Aspidistra elatior 'Asahi'
Glass vases by L'Anverre (Belgium)

211
Ranunculus asiaticus cv.
Xanthorrhoea sp.
Glass vases by L'Anverre (Belgium)

212
Clematis sp.
Xanthorrhoea sp.
Glass vase

213
Above left:
Cornus alba 'Sibirica'
Leontochir ovallei
Glass vase

Above right:
Xanthorrhoea sp.
Zantedeschia sp.

Below left:
Equisetum hyemale
Osmunda japonica

Below right:
Leaves of Hedera
Lilium sp.
Salix sp.

214-15
Oxypetalum caeruleum
Salix sp.
Vase by L'Anverre (Belgium)

216
Eustoma exaltatum subsp.
   russellianum
Lathyrus sp.
Lathyrus odoratus
   'Antique Green'
Salix sp.

217
Pinus palustris

218-19
Epidendrum sp.
Magnolia grandiflora
Vase by L'Anverre (Belgium)

220
Eustoma sp.
Eustoma grandiflora
   'Marron Brown'
Ferns
Lathyrus odoratus cv.
Salix sp.

221
Cornus alba 'Winter Flame'
Ranunculus asiaticus cv.

222
Camellia sp.
Cornus alba 'Sibirica'
Crystal vase by Baccarat (France)

223
Camellia sp.
Clivia sp.
Cornus alba 'Sibirica'
Crystal vase by Baccarat (France)

224
Magnolia grandiflora
Zygopetalum sp.

225
Arisaema sp.
Xanthorrhoea sp.

226
Allium sativum var. ophioscorodon
Leaves of Iris sp.

227
Left:
Paphiopedilum sp.
Zingiber sp.
Vase by Baccarat (France)

Right:
Allium sativum var. ophioscorodon
Xanthorrhoea sp.
Vase by Baccarat (France)

228
Cornus sanguinea 'Viridissima'
Gloriosa sp.

229
Cornus sanguinea 'Viridissima'
Cyrtanthus sp.
Lycaste sp.
Crystal vase by Baccarat (France)

230
Lachenalia viridis
Salix alba 'Tristis'

231
Clematis viridis
Gloriosa sp.
Salix sp.

232-33
Lachenalia viridis
Leucobryum glaucum

234
Above left:
Hedera sp.
Papaver nudicaule
Salix sp.

Above right:
Ranunculus asiaticus cv.
Salix babylonica var. pekinensis
   'Tortuosa'

Below left:
Ranunculus asiaticus cv.
Salix sp.

Below right:
Cornus sanguinea 'Viridissima'
Gerbera sp.
Hedera sp.

235
Eighty varieties of flowers
   and leaves

236
Phalaenopsis sp.

237
Calathea 'Bicajoux'

238
Cornus 'Winter Flame'
Leucobryum glaucum

239
Cornus sanguinea 'Viridissima'
Gloriosa sp.
Vanda sp.

240
Alcantarea 'Purple Skotak'
Phyllostachys edulis
Vanda sp.

241
Bromelia
Split Phyllostachys edulis
Vanda sp.

242
Chrysanthemum sp.
Phyllostachys edulis
Walnut disk by Bernard Duthoy
   (Belgium)

243
Left:
Autumn leaves
Vanda sp.
Vase by Kenichi Nagakura (Japan)

Right:
Split Phyllostachys edulis
Vanda sp.
Vase by Kenichi Nagakura (Japan)

244-45
Spathiphyllum sp.
Typha

246
Phyllostachys edulis

247
Paeonia suffruticosa
Straw

248-49
Juniperus chinensis 'Kaizuka'
Leucobryum glaucum
Wood of Prunus persica
Floral foam

250
Cryptomeria japonica
Juniperus chinensis
Leucobryum glaucum
Phyllostachys edulis

251
Needles of Cryptomeria japonica

252
Above:
Clematis sp.
Capsules of Nelumbo nucifera
Phyllostachys edulis

Below left and right:
Cydonia
Helianthus
Capsules of Nelumbo nucifera
Sarracenia
Vase by Sawa (Germany)

253
Clematis sp.
Phyllostachys edulis

254
Pinus palustris

255
Cryptomeria japonica
Phalaenopsis sp.

256-57
Phyllostachys edulis

258
Anemone sp.
Chrysanthemum sp.
Twenty kinds of mosses
Paeonia sp.
Paeonia suffruticosa cv.
Primula auricula 'Cocoa'
Ranunculus asiaticus cv.
Viburnum opulus
Plexiglas
Rocks

259
Chrysanthemum sp.
Gerbera 'Pasta'
Ranunculus asiaticus cv.
Plexiglas

260-61
Chrysanthemum sp.
Gerbera 'Pasta"
Paeonia sp.
Primula auricula 'Cocoa'
Ranunculus asiaticus cv.
Viburnum opulus
Plexiglas
Rocks

262-63
Phyllostachys edulis

264
Lathyrus odoratus
  'Antique Green'
Salix babylonica

265
Fifty kinds of flowers and
  various green material
Stone vase (more than
  three hundred years old)

266
Split *Phyllostachys edulis*

267
Cornus sanguinea 'Viridissima'
Oncidium sp.
Phalaenopsis sp.

268-69
Equisetum hyemale
Euonymus alatus
Paeonia suffruticosa

270
Above:
Cornus sanguinea 'Viridissima'
Cymbidium 'Black Wind'

Below:
Cornus sanguinea 'Viridissima'
Lathyrus 'Olive Green'

271
Cornus sanguinea 'Viridissima'
Ranunculus asiaticus cv.

272
Euonymus alatus
Lachenalia sp.

273
Euonymus alatus
Lathyrus odoratus 'Antique Green'
Sand

274-75
Leucobryum glaucum
Berries of *Viburnum tinus*
Laser-cut foam

276-77
Cryptomeria japonica
Odontioda sp.
Oncidium sp.

278
Lathyrus odoratus
Pinus palustris
Table by Bernard Duthoy
  (Belgium)

279
Fritillaria camschatcensis
Helleborus orientalis cv.
Japanese ceramic vase

280
Vanda sp.
Colored sticks
Glass

282
Asparagus densiflorus
  'Myriocladus'
Gypsophila paniculata
Floral foam

285
Bromelia
Artificial grass by Domo

286-87
Adiantum raddianum
Phalaenopsis sp.
Sphagnum moss

288-89
Rhododendron indicum

290-91
Gloriosa superba cv.
Phyllostachys edulis
Burned *Phyllostachys edulis*

292
Branches of *Actinidia chinensis*
Castanea sativa
Phyllostachys edulis

293
Peel of *Citrus* sp.
Glass vase by L'Anverre (Belgium)

294-95
Dahlia sp.
Eustoma sp.
Gerbera sp.
Hydrangea sp.

296
Hyacinthus orientalis cv.
Xanthorrhoea sp.

297
Phyllostachys edulis
Zantedeschia

298-301
Grass
Hydrangea paniculata
  'Pinky-Winky'
Laurus nobilis
Verbena sp.

302
Japanese fruit
Juniperus sp.

303
Foliage of *Buxus* or *Ilex*
  and other variants
Rosa cv.

304-5
Asparagus
Rosa cv.
Smilax japonica

306-7
Asparagus
Foliage of *Buxus* or *Ilex*
Rosa cv.

308
Grass
Laurus nobilis
Verbena 'Thalys Cream White'

309
Anthurium sp.
Salix sp.
Verbena 'Kimono Red'

310
Euphorbia fulgens

311
Gerbera sp.

312
Achillea filipendulina cv.
Bougainvillea glabra cv.
Fuchsia sp.
Ixora sp.
Rosa 'Sahara'
Vanda sp.
Cotton and pigment
Various branches

313
Asparagus setaceus
Phalaenopsis sp.

314-15
Lathyrus odoratus

316
Fragaria × *magna*
Hordeum
Olea europaea

317
Paeonia 'Coral Charm'
Paeonia 'Coral Sunset'
Phyllostachys edulis

318
Petals of *Rosa* cv.

319
Cornus alba 'Sibirica'

320
Split *Phyllostachys edulis*

321
Chrysanthemum sp.
Rosa cv.

322-23
Gypsophila sp.

324
Dendrobium sp.
Phalaenopsis sp.

325
Dendrobium sp.

326
Laurus nobilis

327
Strelitzia reginae

328-29
Gypsophila paniculata
Paeonia sp.
Rosa cv.
Zantedeschia 'Crystal Blush'

330
Rhododendron indicum

331
Rhododendron indicum

332
Above:
Hydrangea macrophylla cv.
Plexiglas

Below:
Eucharis grandiflora
Eustoma sp.
Lathyrus odoratus cv.
Rosa cv.

333
Above:
Dendrobium 'Okinawa'
Gypsophila
Phyllostachys edulis

Below:
Phyllostachys edulis
Xanthorrhoea sp.
Vanda sp.

334
Rosa cv.

335
Buxus
Citrus
Rosa cv.

336
Aquilegia sp.
Campanula sp.
Dicentra spectabilis
Nigella sp.
Wild grass

337
Branches of *Cornus nuttallii*
Tree peonies
Faux bois

338-41
Kalanchoe sp.

342-43
Bougainvillea sp.
Vanda sp.
Painted sticks

344
Rosa cv.

345
Begonia sp.
Rocks

346-47
Bromelia sp.
Phyllostachys edulis
Vanda sp.

348
Cymbidium
Leaves of *Iris* sp.

350
Buxus sp.
Eustoma sp.
Malus
Rosa cv.

353
Berries of *Coffea* sp.
Leaves of *Magnolia grandiflora*

354
Cornus alba 'Sibirica'
Malus

355
Oncidium sp.
Phyllostachys nigra

356
Betula sp.
Various spring flowers

357
Euphorbia pulcherrima
Leucobryum glaucum
Phyllostachys edulis
Rice grains

358
Salix sp.

359
Branches
Leucobryum glaucum
Mushrooms

360-61
Buttercups
Camellia
Nerine
Rosa cv.
Varied foliage

362
Above:
Ixia sp.
Leucojum vernum
Xerophyllum tenax

Below:
Cymbidium
Leaves of *Iris* sp.

363
Above:
Eustoma sp.
Ferns
Lathyrus odoratus cv.
Rosa cv.
Salix sp.

Below:
Paeonia suffruticosa cv.

364
Allium sativum var. *ophioscorodon*
Leucojum aestivum
Phyllostachys edulis

365
Aspidistra elatior
Convallaria majalis
Galanthus nivalis
Leucojum aestivum
Stephanotis floribunda
Xerophyllum tenax

366
Clematis montana
Xanthorrhoea sp.

367
Aspidistra elatior 'Asahi'
Xanthorrhoea sp.

368-69
Adiantum
Hydrangea sp.
Nigella sp.
Varied foliage

370
Bromelia sp.
Phyllostachys edulis
Rosa cv.

371
Buxus
Ilex verticillata
Rosa 'Ivanhoe'
Rosa cv.

372
Leucobryum glaucum
Needles and bark of *Pinus nigra*

373
Berries of *Ilex verticillata*
Leaves of *Populus alba* 'Nivea'

374
Above left:
Nelumbo nucifera
Glass vase by B&B Italia (Italy)

Above right:
Aspidistra elatior 'Asahi'
Tulipa sp.

Below left:
Nelumbo nucifera
Vase by L'Anverre (Belgium)

Below right:
Nelumbo nucifera
Ceramics by B&B Italia (Italy)

375
Aspidistra elatior 'Asahi'
Ceramics by B&B Italia (Italy)

376
Cotinus coggygria
Paeonia sp.
Shoots of *Phyllostachys edulis*

377
Cotinus coggygria
Paeonia sp.
Shoots of *Phyllostachys edulis*
Vase by Domani (Belgium)

378
Cotinus coggygria
Eustoma 'Mango'
Shoots of *Phyllostachys edulis*
Vase by Domani (Belgium)

379
Cotinus coggygria
Eustoma 'Mango'
Vases by L'Anverre (Belgium)

380
Curcuma sp.
Crystal vase by Baccarat (France)

381
Leaves of *Anthurium crystallinum*
Grapes
Melon
Zinnia

382
Clematis sp.
Cornus sanguinea 'Viridissima'
Fritillaria sp.

383
Above:
Aechmea aquilegia
Anthurium crystallinum
Bromelia
Eustoma exaltatum subsp.
   russellianum
Fern leaves

Below:
Cotinus coggygria
Disa uniflora
Vase by Domani (Belgium)

384-85
Shoots of *Phyllostachys edulis*
Split *Phyllostachys edulis*

386
Cornus alba 'Sibirica'
Sarracenia sp.

391
Coleus blumei cv.

392
Pinus palustris
Rosa 'Marie-Anne'

395
Eustoma grandiflora cv.
Gladiolus sp.
Lathyrus odoratus cv.
Magnolia sp.
Vase by Domani (Belgium)

397
Gladiolus sp.
Scirpus sp.
Bronze vase by Hanamasa
   (Japan)

400
Equisetum hyemale
Iris ensata
Ophiopogon

403
Clematis sp.

A mosaic of painted nettle, *Coleus*, overlays
the grass of the Antwerp Zoo and evokes
the skin pattern of a giraffe.

BIOGRAPHY OF DANIEL OST

PLANTS AS A MEANS OF EXPRESSION

Daniel Ost was born in 1955 in Sint-Niklaas, Belgium, where he still lives and works. He is married to Marie-Anne and together they have two children, Maarten and Nele. Ost owns flower shops in Sint-Niklaas and in Brussels, and in 2016 he will open a flower academy in Japan, his second homeland.

"Flowers and plants have always been a part of my being," he wrote in *Leafing Through Flowers I (Bladeren in Bloemen I)*. "My work with them is not the result of study, but rather of an innate interest. My early childhood years, spent with my grandparents, plunged me prematurely into the world of soil, roots, stems, and petals that my grandfather cultivated. It was he who awoke this budding curiosity." Ost often tells the story of how, at age three, he fell into a well of manure while trying to pluck a rose. When he was dragged out, unconscious, he was still holding the rose firmly in his little hand.

His father was not pleased with this love of flowers, which he viewed as a woman's avocation, so he sent his son to a military academy in an attempt to redirect his interests. But Ost was undeterred and remained impassioned about flowers and plants. When he turned nineteen, he decided to follow his own path. He briefly considered studying cabaret in the Netherlands, but

A still life with a rose is titled *Marie-Anne,* after Ost's wife.

the flowers were calling. Fate helped him on occasion: "In life you need a certain amount of luck. You can have the talent and the drive, but sometimes you have to meet the right people at the right time." At just this moment, the Dutch flower designer Peter Curfs opened a flower shop in Sint-Niklaas, and Ost was fascinated by what he saw there. One day he worked up the courage to ask whether he could help out in the shop. Curfs taught him not only the craft, but also that flowers and plants could become one's personal means of artistic expression. He followed a master's training in flower arrangement in Vught, the Netherlands, and in 1979 won the Belgian floral arrangement championship. Over the following years, he reaped countless awards in competitions in Belgium, the Netherlands, and Germany, and took second prize at the world championship in Detroit, Michigan, in 1985.

In 1983 Ost visited Japan for the first time. In a Tokyo shop he discovered a beautiful photo book by Noboru Kurisaki, tea master and one of the most prominent ikebana grand masters. Ost inquired about visiting his shop, not realizing that Kurisaki was the owner of Nishi-no-Ki, a very exclusive private club in Roppongi, and a meeting place for Tokyo's artistic elite and gay jet set. When Ost visited Kurisaki a few days later, a new world opened up to him in the shop. Never before had he seen so many flowers at once, such a fabulous collection of art nouveau vases, such opulent interiors. Kurisaki was reserved at first, but he was soon swayed by the floral passion of the young Fleming. It was the beginning of a lifelong friendship and of Ost's fascination with Japan and the Far East. "Kurisaki opened my eyes and played a decisive role in the development of my aesthetic sense and my design lexicon," he says. "He once told me: 'Daniel-san, sometimes a single flower says more than ten thousand flowers.'"

In the late 1980s, Ost met Martine De Clerck of the DOMO textile manufacturing group. Overwhelmed by his floral compositions and unusual talent, she convinced him to create a book of his work. He labored over the project for a year, making hundreds of new compositions, often at special locations, letting his fantasy and creativity run wild. *Leafing Through Flowers I* was released in 1989. It would be the first volume in a long series. Thanks in part to that publication, he was invited to enter the world championship of flower decoration in Osaka, where he won first prize. Since then, he has exhibited dozens of times in Japan at exclusive locations, and he is a genuine celebrity there.

In 1991 the Belgian royal house commissioned Ost to supply the floral decorations for the "40/60 celebrations" of King Baudouin (referring to the coincident fortieth anniversary of the king's accession to the throne and his sixtieth birthday). This led him to create one of his first showpieces at Heysel Stadium in Brussels: a gigantic canopy covered in fine maidenhair and ornamented with nine thousand white orchids, above a pond with Victoria water lilies. Over the years he would work repeatedly for the Belgian royal house, creating the floral arrangements and sculptures for the weddings of Crown Prince Philippe in 1999 and Prince Laurent in 2003.

Thanks to his books, the royal commissions, and his phenomenal success in Japan, his star continued to rise. He has been called upon in Japan, Korea, the Persian Gulf States, Russia, France, Italy, and the United States for countless events. A few years ago the cover of the French magazine *Paris Match* declared him "the international star of floral decoration." "The Van Gogh of flower decoration" he has been called in Japan. "The Picasso of flower arranging" he was described in the Belgian newspaper *La Libre Belgique.*

Yet what Ost does with flowers and plants—indeed, with all conceivable vegetable materials—defies the imagination and has little to do with traditional flower arranging. "What do you call what Daniel Ost creates?" asks the Dutch writer Cees Nooteboom in his essay in this

This classic-looking composition, with fanciful
magnolia branches in bud, is inspired by the colors
of the vase. Less traditional is the enormous scope
of the work: the vase with the *acanthus* motif is a
yard high, and the entire composition stands more
than three yards tall.

volume. Ost's work is sometimes compared with that of the contemporary artists Lucio Fontana, Anish Kapoor, and Claes Oldenburg, or with land artists, such as Andy Goldsworthy and Richard Long. He dismisses these comparisons, although he acknowledges his deep admiration for these artists. He prefers to see himself as a flower designer.

In recent years Ost has also begun designing gardens. They offer the ideal counterpart to the ephemeral and often very stressful and physically demanding work with cut flowers. "A garden is something that remains," he says. "It also grows and evolves. With my floral design work, the concept is entirely in my head and the result is immediately visible. With a garden, I have to keep thinking about how it will look years from now. That is very exciting." What started out as a favor for a neighbor has grown into a new passion—and in this field, too, his fame is fast spreading.

Schoolchildren gaze at a composition
of bulrush, or *Scirpus*, decorated
with Japanese gladiolas in an antique
bronze vase.

CHRONOLOGY
EXHIBITIONS AND EVENTS

1979
Winner, Belgian Flower Cup
Brussels, Belgium

1979
Exhibition:
Bundesgartenschau
Bonn, Germany

1979
Exhibition: *Flowers & Animals*
Antwerp, Belgium

1981
Winner, Golden Orchid Cup
Hannover, Germany

1981
Exhibition: *People
& Landscape*
Antwerp, Belgium

1981
Opening: Shop
Sint-Niklaas, Belgium

1982
Decoration: Erasmus
Foundation Charity Party
La Hulpe, Belgium

1982
Exhibition: *People & Space*
Antwerp, Belgium

1982
International Lecture Tour
Asia (Taiwan, Japan, China,
Thailand), USA

1983
Decoration: Erasmus
Foundation Charity Party
La Hulpe, Belgium

1983
Winner, Belgian Flower Cup
Brussels, Belgium

1983
Second Place, European
Championship
Brussels, Belgium

1984
Decoration: Erasmus
Foundation Charity Party
La Hulpe, Belgium

1985
Decoration: Erasmus
Foundation Charity Party
La Hulpe, Belgium

1985
Second Place, World
Championship
Detroit, MI, USA

1986
Decoration: Erasmus
Foundation Charity Party
La Hulpe, Belgium

1987
Decoration: Erasmus
Foundation Charity Party
La Hulpe, Belgium

1988
Decoration: Erasmus
Foundation Charity Party
La Hulpe, Belgium

1989
Decoration: Erasmus
Foundation Charity Party
La Hulpe, Belgium

1990
Winner, Osaka Flower Expo
Osaka, Japan

1990
Decoration: Erasmus
Foundation Charity Party
La Hulpe, Belgium

1990
Decoration:
Celebrations of King
Baudouin
Brussels, Belgium

1991
Decoration: Erasmus
Foundation Charity Party
La Hulpe, Belgium

1992
Decoration: Erasmus
Foundation Charity Party
La Hulpe, Belgium

1993
Decoration: Erasmus
Foundation Charity Party
La Hulpe, Belgium

1993
World Tour of Flower
Demonstrations
Asia (Japan, Hong Kong,
Taiwan) and Europe (Italy,
Sweden, Norway, Germany,
France)

1994
Decoration: Erasmus
Foundation Charity Party
La Hulpe, Belgium

1995
Decoration: Erasmus
Foundation Charity Party
La Hulpe, Belgium

1995
Decoration: Belgian Consulate
Hong Kong

1996
Demonstration Tour
Japan

1996
Decoration: Erasmus
Foundation Charity Party
La Hulpe, Belgium

1996
Nogakudo Charity
Demonstration
Tokyo, Japan

1997
Exhibition: *Ise-Shima
Pearl Project*
Ise-Shima, Japan

1997
Decoration: Erasmus
Foundation Charity Party
La Hulpe, Belgium

1997
Exhibition: *Autumn,*
Sugimoto Residence
Kyoto, Japan

1998
Christmas Decoration:
Four Seasons Hotel
Tokyo, Japan

1998
Decoration: Erasmus
Foundation Charity Party
La Hulpe, Belgium

1998
Opening: Christie's
Rockefeller Plaza Office
New York, NY, USA

1999
Decoration: Wedding
of Crown Prince Philippe
of Belgium
Brussels, Belgium

1999
Decoration: Belgian Pavilion
at the Horticultural Expo
Kunming, China

1999
Decoration: Erasmus
Foundation Charity Party
La Hulpe, Belgium

1999
Decoration: Mark Rothko
Retrospective
Paris, France

2000
Exhibition: *Bird of Flowers*
Osaka Table Art Fair
Osaka, Japan

2000
Exhibition: *Kanazawa
Noh Theater*
Kanazawa, Japan

2000
Decoration: Erasmus
Foundation Charity Party
La Hulpe, Belgium

2000
Decoration: Immokalee
Foundation
Naples, FL, USA

2001
Decoration: Erasmus
Foundation Charity Party
La Hulpe, Belgium

2001
Decoration: Opening
of Christie's
Paris, France

2002
Exhibition: *Spring,*
Sugimoto Residence
Kyoto, Japan

2002
Decoration: Erasmus
Foundation Charity Party
La Hulpe, Belgium

2002
Decoration: Society of Four
Arts Reopening
Palm Beach, FL, USA

2003
Decoration: Wedding of
Prince Laurent of Belgium
Brussels, Belgium

2003
Opening: Shop
Brussels, Belgium

2003
Decoration: Erasmus
Foundation Charity Party
La Hulpe, Belgium

2003
Wedding Show, Hotel Nikko
Tokyo, Japan

2004
Decoration: Wedding
of a Member of the Royal
Family of Jordan
Petra, Jordan

2004
Exhibition: Gana Art Gallery
Seoul, South Korea

2004
Exhibition: Ninna-ji
Kyoto, Japan

2004
Exhibition: Tsunamachi
Mitsui Club
Tokyo, Japan

2004
Exhibition: *Moon Garden*
Pacific Flora
Hamamatsu, Japan

2004
Decoration: Erasmus
Foundation Charity Party
La Hulpe, Belgium

2004
Design of Six Special Coca-
Cola Bottles: Flower to the
People

2005
Wedding Show, Hotel Okura
Kobe, Japan

2005
Decoration: Celebration
of 50 Years of Diplomatic
Relations Between Belgium
and India
Mumbai, India

2005
Decoration: Belgian Pavilion,
Aichi Expo
Aichi, Japan

2005
Exhibition: Sogetsu Hall
Tokyo, Japan

2005
Christmas Decoration:
Shiseido
Tokyo, Japan

2005
Decoration: Conrad Hotel
Opening
Tokyo, Japan

2005
Exhibition: Tour & Taxis
Brussels, Belgium

2005
Winner, Ghent Floralies
Ghent, Belgium

2005
Decoration: Erasmus
Foundation Charity Party
La Hulpe, Belgium

2006
Decoration: Marshall Field's
and Bachman's Spring
Flower Show
Minneapolis, MN, USA

2006
Decoration: Royal Wedding
Abu Dhabi, UAE

2006
Decoration: Dries Van Noten
Fashion Show
Paris, France

2006
Exhibition: *Experience Days and Lexus Nights*
Brussels, Belgium

2006
Exhibition: *Autumn* Commemorating the 1,200th Anniversary of Kobo-Daishi's Return to Japan, Tō-ji
Kyoto, Japan

2006
Winner, Chiang Mai Royal Flora (Representing Belgium)
Chiang Mai, Thailand

2006
Christmas Decoration: Imperial Hotel Plaza
Tokyo, Japan

2006
Decoration: Palazzo Grassi Museum Opening
Venice, Italy

2006
Decoration: Arsenale
Venice, Italy

2006
Decoration: Erasmus Foundation Charity Party
La Hulpe, Belgium

2007
Decoration: Erasmus Foundation Charity Party
La Hulpe, Belgium

2007
Exhibition: Shibuya Seibu
Shibuya, Japan

2007
Exhibition: *Spring*
Tō-ji
Kyoto, Japan

2007
Decoration: Erasmus Foundation Charity Party
La Hulpe, Belgium

2007
Exhibition: *Daniel Ost's Cosmos*
Sogo Shinsaibashi
Osaka, Japan

2007
Exhibition: *Daniel Ost: Nocturne*
Tour & Taxis
Brussels, Belgium

2007
Christmas Decoration: Imperial Hotel Plaza
Tokyo, Japan

2007
Spring Decoration: Imperial Hotel Plaza
Tokyo, Japan

2007
Exhibition: *Daniel Ost: Roses*
Sint-Niklaas, Belgium

2007
Design: Laurent-Perrier Gardens at the Tuileries
Paris, France

2007
Decoration: Fondazione Giorgio Cini
Venice, Italy

2008
Decoration: Wedding of His Highness the Crown Prince of Qatar
Doha, Qatar

2008
Exhibition: *Daniel Ost: Royal Wedding*
Imperial Hotel
Tokyo, Japan

2008
Exhibition: Seibu Ikebukuro
Tokyo, Japan

2008
Decoration: Museum of Islamic Art Opening
Doha, Qatar

2008
Decoration: Royal Park Rajapruek
Chiang Mai, Thailand

2008
Exhibition: *Daniel Ost: Royal Wedding*
Imperial Hotel Plaza
Tokyo, Japan

2008
Exhiibition: *Daniel Ost at Home*
Salons of Fine Arts
Sint-Niklaas, Belgium

2008
Decoration: Erasmus Foundation Charity Party
La Hulpe, Belgium

2009
Exhibition: Takashimaya
Tokyo, Japan

2009
Exhibition: Kinkaku-ji
Kyoto, Japan

2009
Christmas Decoration: Imperial Hotel Plaza
Tokyo, Japan

2009
Christmas Decoration: Lexus and Daiichi-Engei
Tokyo, Japan

2009
Exhibition: Landcommanderij Alden Biesen
Bilzen, Belgium

2009
Exhibition: The Heizel
Brussels, Belgirum

2009
Christmas Decoration: Town Hall
Sint-Niklaas, Belgium

2009
Wedding: Member of the Royal Family of Abu Dhabi
Abu Dhabi, UAE

2009
Decoration: Erasmus Foundation Charity Party
La Hulpe, Belgium

2010
Exhibition: *Daniel Ost: Microcosmos*
Seibu Ikebukuro
Tokyo, Japan

2010
Design: Laurent-Perrier and Chanel Rooftop Garden
Tokyo, Japan

2010
Winner, Ghent Floralies
Ghent, Belgium

2010
Exhibition: Laurel on the Market
Bruges, Belgium

2010
Decoration: Hotel Imperial Plaza
Tokyo, Japan

2010
Decoration: Erasmus Foundation Charity Party
La Hulpe, Belgium

2010
Decoration: Town Hall
Sint-Niklaas, Belgium

2011
Flower Installation: Tsunamachi Mitsui Club
Tokyo, Japan

2011
Exhibition: *Roses for Coloma* with Fashion Designer Kaat Tilley
Brussels, Belgium

2011
Exhibition: The Heizel
Brussels, Belgium

2011
Decoration: Erasmus Foundation Charity Party
La Hulpe, Belgium

2012
Exhibition: *Daniel Ost: Theatre* Floriade
Almere, the Netherlands

2012
Exhibition: *Reflections 775* Roosenberg Abbey
Waasmunster, Belgium

2012
Wedding: Member of the Royal Family of Saudi Arabia
Riyadh, Saudi Arabia

2012
Exhibition: *Splendid Table Decorations*
Matsuzakaya
Nagoya, Japan

2012
Exhibition: 20th Anniversary of the Japanese Garden
Hasselt, Belgium

2012
Exhibition: Flower Extravaganza, Central Chidlom
Bangkok, Thailand

2012
Christmas Decoration: 111th Anniversary of Bergdorf Goodman
New York, NY, USA

2012
Decoration: Bergdorf Goodman Fashion Week
New York, NY, USA

2012
Christmas Decoration: Hotel Seiyo Ginza
Tokyo, Japan

2012
Decoration: Belfry of Bruges
Belgium

2012
Invitation: Royal Trade Mission to Japan with His Highness Prince Philippe of Belgium
Tokyo, Japan

2012
Decoration: Belgian Embassy
Tokyo, Japan

2012
Exhibition: *A Prayer of Flowers* Higashi-Matsushima Temple
Higashimatsushima, Japan

2013
Exhibition: Daniel Ost and Yawatagaki, Izumo-taisha Grand Shrine Heisei
Izumo, Japan

2013
Decoration: Tomorrowland Music Festival
Antwerp, Belgium

2013
Floral Design Workshop
Colares, Portugal

2014
Decoration: Tomorrowland Music Festival
Antwerp, Belgium

2014
Decoration: Wedding of His Highness the Crown Prince of Abu Dhabi
Abu Dhabi, UAE

2014
Opening: Daniel Ost Flower Academy
Sint-Niklaas, Belgium

2015
Exhibition: *The Most Beautiful Flower Story*
Miyazaki, Japan

2015
Exhibition: *Daniel Ost in Kurashiki*
Ôhara Residence and Museum
Kurashiki, Japan

2015
Decoration: Tomorrowland Music Festival
Antwerp, Belgium

2015
Featured in the German Magazine *Luxus Garten* as One of Europe's Best Garden Designers

2015
Exhibition: *Discover the Undiscovered*
Tour & Taxis
Brussels, Belgium

2015
Appointed Designer of a Postage Stamp for the British Royal Mail in Memory of World War I
London, England

2015
Appointed Head Garden and Floral Designer for Alon Las Vegas Resort
Nevada, USA

ACKNOWLEDGMENTS

Mr. & Mrs. Pramod Agarwal, Agora, Yoko Aihara, Takuya Akai, Tomoko Akama, Alexandra Alexandrova, Saif Al Gandy, His Highness Dr. Sheikh Sultan bin Khalifa Al Nahyan, His Highness Sheikh Tahnoon bin Mohammed Al Nahyan, Abdullah Al Najar, Yoshiaki Amano, Anco Orchids, Tage Anderson, Masuo Ando, Olga Andreeva, Keiko Aono, Megumi Araki, Arboretum Kalmthout, Raitei Arima, Kazuyo Asayama, Avalane, B&B Italia, Baccarat Pacific, Preston Bailey, Manu Beers, Michiel Beers, Gerda Benoit, Bruno Bernaerts, Mr. & Mrs. Bloch George, Mayya Bobrova, Pierre Boon, Nico Bosteels, Botanic Garden Meise, Jean-Baptiste Bourrat, Bob Bridts, Asselien Broekhuis, Pelageya Budankova, Anna Burova, Isaburo Cadeau, Yann Callaert, Els Caruso, Bertrand Catrysse, Champagne Laurent-Perrier, Hyeran Choi, Minyi Choi, Christie's (Paris), Ben Clevers, Mrs. Henri Clijsters, Mr. & Mrs. Miles C. Collier, Conrad Tokyo Hotel, Jeroen Coorman, Frank Coupé, Dai-ichi Seed Co., Ltd., Daitoku-ji, Hitomi Date, Marie-Clotilde De Bieuvre, Mr. & Mrs. Jan De Clerck-Van den Weghe, Mr. & Mrs. Jozef De Cock, Chantal De Keersmaeker, Ignace De Paepe, Nele De Ryck, Eric De Vos, De Wolf BVBA, Mr. & Mrs. René Denis, Deroose Plants NV, Mr. & Mrs. André Devisch, Robert Dewilde, Frans D'Haese, Mr. & Mrs. Guy D'Haese, Mr. & Mrs. Jozef & Jeanine Dockx, Anne-Laure Domenichini, Mr. & Mrs. Marcel Dubourg, Bernard Duthoy, Eccentric / Mr. Demey, Naji Elmahi, Cedric Etienne, Maria Ferrari, Flanders Center (Osaka), Flora Korea, Fondazione Giorgio Cini (Venice), Fonds Erasme pour la Recherche Médicale (Brussels), Four Seasons Hotel Chinzanso, Martien Franck, Charlotte M. Frieze, Fujisaki Office Co., Ltd., Fujisankei Living Services, Ltd., Shusaku Fujita, Atsushi Fujiwara, Takako Furuya, Galerie Orphée / M. Takashi Suzuki, Carla Galle, Gana Art Gallery Seoul, Laurent Germeau, Philippe Gernay, Hamanaka Gesson, Sylvia Goldschmidt, Pierre Grégoire, Yulia Guseva, Nanako Hagiwara, Saebyul Ham, Satoko Hamamura, Emiko Harada, Meiko Harada, Masahiro Hashizume, Kyoko Hayama, Ruud Hazelaar, Hermès (Tokyo), Michiko Hirata, Kayoko Hirota, Shinobu Hisaki, Mrs. Hofkens, Masako Hongo, Mrs. Eriko Horiki & Associates, Collin Hotermans, ID&T Belgium, Hanabishi Ligo Katuhito, Seibu Ikebukuro, Imperial Hotel Tokyo, Yoshie Ino, Daisuke Isamoto, Eiko Ishikawa, Fumiko Ishikawa, Hiroko Ito, Julia Ito, Keiko Ito, Masahiro Ito, Eunok Jang, Mr. & Mrs. Freddy Janssens, Jenwit family, Yutaka Jimbo, André Joyeux, Katsunori Kanda, Keiko Kaneko, Emi Kanno, Noriko Kashiwagi, Eva Kasparkova, Junichi Kawamura, Mami Kawasaki, Hirota Kayoko, Hirata Kenichiro, Kenrokuen, Tomoyo Kikisui, Hiroko Kikuchi, Doyoun Kim, Yuki Kimura, Keiko Kitashirakawa, Kuniko Kito, Hiroko Kobayashi, Hiroshi Kobayashi, Mieko Kodama, Takahiro Kondo, Yoichiro Kori, Natsuko Koriyama, Natalia Korotina, Kurashiki prefecture, Nobura Kurisaki, Kenji Kusakabe, Satoshi Kusakabe, Yoshiki Kuwahara, Ekatarina Kuzmina, Tō-ji, Dirk Laeremans, Matthias Lannoo, L'Anverre, Mr. & Mrs. Xavier Laporta, Lauretum Jabbeke, Laurica Plants, Annie Lernout, Lexus Belgium, Viviane Leyman, Mr. & Mrs. Luc Liebaut, Roger Liekens, Mr. & Mrs. Steve Lin, Mr. & Mrs. Jean Machiels, Reiko Maeda, Jan Maenhout, Henk Mahieu, Elena Makeeva, Mandarin Oriental Hotel Bangkok, Chris Martens, Jan Martens, Susuki Masao, Mr. & Mrs. Sirin Masri, Marcel Massa, Mariko Masuda, Kyoko Matsuda, Keiko Matsumoto, Masanori Matsuura, Kenichi Matsuyama, Ken Matsuzaki, Tou Matsuzaki, Media Network Inc., Tokyo, Rushmi Mehta and family, Stéphanie Meneux de Nonancourt, Jos Mertens, Mechtild Mes, Family de Mevius, Yoji Mihara, Taeko Millet, Mr. & Mrs. Lakshmi Mittal, Bunryo Miura, Masaki Miyano, Mariko Mochikawa, Professor Yoko Mori, Hiroko Morinaga, Seiki Muta, Yoshiko Nagae, Kenichi Nagakura, Yuri Nagao, Miki Nagura, Toshiharu Nakagawa, Kaoni Nakajima, Kaoru Nakajima, Kiyokazu Nakajima, Takuo Nakamura, Takumi Nakaya, Reiko Nakayama, NHK Enterprises Inc., Ninna-Ji, Tamiko Nishi, Yasukazu Nishihata, Yudai Nishihata, Yoshiko Nishimura, Fumiko Nishino, Shizuko Nishino, Rieko Nishio, Keiko Niwa, Maki Nonoguchi, Noritake Japan, Fukuko Norizuki, Hatsumi Ogawa, Taketoshi Ogawa, Hinako Oguchi, Kenichiro Ōhara, Toshio Ohi, Kazuo Oka, Oichiro Oka, Yasuko Okamoto, Yaeko Okawa, Etsuko Okumura, Jan Oprins, Maarten Ost, Nele Ost, Naomi Onuki, Yukio Otani, Aleksandr Otlivanchik, Damien Overputte, Izumo Oyashiro, Bruno Pani, Park Hyatt Tokyo, Patek Philippe, Juliette de Patoul, Alexandra Pereyre de Nonancourt, Petrakis family, Phaidon Press, Phoenix Seagaia Resort, Roeland Pieterszoon D'Haese, Jan Pillen, Mr. & Mrs. François Pinault, Plant Partners Inc., Profirst, the Qatar Museums Authority, Frank Ranson, Khun Reed, Royal Copenhagen, the Royal Family of Abu Dhabi, the Royal Family of Belgium, the Royal Family of Dubai, the Royal Family of Qatar, Royal Society for Agriculture and Botany (Gand), Sangmi Ryu, Masako Saito, Fusako Sakai, Yukari Sakai, Yoshie Sakuragi, Friedrich-Karl & Elisabeth Sandmann, Jun Sato, Sueyo Satomi, Kiyotsugu Sawa, Kunei Sazuka, Yvonne Schuurmans, Seibundo Shinkosha, Takamasa Senge, Seibu Tokyo, Reika Shibata, Machiko Shimada, Kanae Shimakawa, Shimane prefecture, Harumi Shimizu, Toshio Shimizu, Noriko Shimura, Nakai Shinji, Shiseido Ltd., Tokyo, Mr. & Mrs. Shoda, Yasuko Shoda, the Sisters of the Roosenberg Abbey, Sino-Thai Corp., Smithers-Oasis Belgium nv, Smithers-Oasis Japan Co., Ltd. / Mr. Toshiro Mori, Sogetsu Plaza Tokyo, Spark Flower Academy, City of Sint-Niklaas, Hilda Stange-Van der Wekken, Usui Sueo, Sugimoto family, Setsuko Sugimoto, Utako Sugimoto, Deco Suzuki, Masao Suzuki, Mutsumi Suzuki, Nobue Suzuki, Sanae Suzuki, Yumi Suzuki, Taché family, Masakazu Taguchi, Midori Tajitsu, Amano Takafumi, Yuko Takaki, Tsuchiya Takako, Yukiko Takamiya, Takashimaya, Nobuyuki Takesada, Yoshiaki Takishima, Emiko Tamaki, Junko Tamaoki, Hiroko Tanaka, Ikuko Tanaka, Kazuhiko Tanaka, Keiko Tanaka, Sanae Tanaka, Tomiya Tanigawa, Yoshie Tanioka, Kazuko Tatano, An Theunynck, Marianne Thys, Kayoko Toda, Tomoe Tokuhiro, Toshio Tomita, Anna Torfs, Hitomi Tsuchiya, Shiro Tsujimura, Kosei Tsukahara, Tsunamachi Mitsui Club, Hisayo Uchiyama, Mr. & Mrs. Guy Ullens de Schooten, Joël Van Audenhaege, Mrs. Van Boxelaere, Dirk Van Den Eynde, Roos Van de Velde, Mr. & Mrs. Johan Vandendriessche, Rudy Van Hoey, Van Hool family, Wies Van Laere, Dries Van Noten, Mr. & Mrs. Luc Van Remoortel, Mrs. Gerd Van Turnhout-Nagels, Marco van Veldhuizen, Mr. & Mrs. Baron Piet van Waeyenberge, Zhumagul Vasilyeva, Olaf Veenhuizen, Mr. & Mrs. Adrien Verdegem, Maarten Verhelst, Toon Verhelst, Anne Vierstraete, Vigilando BVBA, Villa Eugénie (Brussels), Villeroy & Boch (Brussels), VLAM, Irina Vodolaszkaya, Nobuko Wakamori, Ludo Willems, WUD Flowers Abu Dhabi, Keiko Yamamoto, Kazuhiro Yamane, Mitsuharu Yane, Mutsuko Yawatagaki, Shiho Yawatagaki, YES, Saeko Yokoe, Takashima Yoshiaki, You-Kaen Inc. / Mr. Youya Yamada & Mrs. Ayumi Yamada, Akiva Zama, Olga Zhuravleva, Zoo Antwerpen and Taisiia Zubrenko.

My team in Belgium and in Japan, all those who helped me over the years and who participated in this book.

Daniel Ost

The "river" in this private garden meanders
its way between carefully selected fragments
of natural stone.

BIBLIOGRAPHY

Ost, Daniel. *Leafing Through Flowers I.* Sint-Niklaas, Belgium: Martine De Clerck–Van den Weghe, 1989.

——. *Leafing Through Flowers II.* Sint-Niklaas, Belgium: Ost Publications, 1993.

——. *Leafing Through Flowers III.* Sint-Niklaas, Belgium: Floreal BVBA, 1997.

——. *Ostentatief.* Tielt, Belgium: Lannoo, 1998.

Ost, Daniel, Jean-Pierre Gabriel, and Robert Dewilde. *Invitations.* Tielt, Belgium: Lannoo-Terra, 2002.

——. *Remaining Flowers.* Tielt, Belgium: Lannoo-Terra, 2003.

Ost, Daniel and Jean-Pierre Gabriel. *East x West.* Sint-Niklaas, Belgium: Floreal BVBA, 2005.

Ost, Daniel. *Transparent.* Tielt, Belgium: Lannoo, 2007.

——. *Daniel Ost in Shibuya Seibu.* Herentals, Belgium: Rekad, 2007.

Ost, Daniel and Jean-Pierre Gabriel. *Invitations II.* Tielt, Belgium: Lannoo-Terra, 2009.

Ost, Daniel. *Daniel Ost in Kyoto.* Kyoto: Fusosha, 2009.

AUTHOR BIOS

PAUL GEERTS

Paul Geerts studied law and sociology in Leuven, Utrecht, and Florence. He has been a freelance journalist and consultant since 2000, specializing in botany, gardens, and landscape architecture. Geerts writes for various Belgian and Dutch publications, and is the author of several books on gardening and trees.

KENGO KUMA

Kengo Kuma studied architecture at the University of Tokyo in 1979, then pursued further training at Columbia University. In 1987 he launched Spatial Design Studio, and in 1990 he founded his architecture firm, Kengo Kuma & Associates. Steeped in Japanese tradition, he seeks to integrate that heritage into his work while giving it a new interpretation. He has lectured at Columbia University, the University of Illinois, and Keio University of Tokyo, where, in 2008, he presented his doctoral thesis. Today he teaches at the Graduate School of Architecture in Tokyo. In 2009, in recognition of his many achievements, he was made an officer of the Ordre des Arts et des Lettres in France.

CEES NOOTEBOOM

Cees Nooteboom is considered one of the most talented contemporary Dutch writers. He has published many books over a careeer spanning more than four decades–from a philosophical novel to poetry, short stories, and travel journals, as well as journalistic essays. Nooteboom divides his time between Amsterdam and the island of Minorca in the Balearic Islands, and has traveled around the world. In 1992 he was elected to the Academy of Arts in Berlin. He has received, among many other awards, the Constantijn Huygens Prize, the P. C. Hooft Prize, and the Dutch Literature Prize; the latter is the most important literary award for writers in the Dutch-speaking world.

PHOTO CREDITS

Jef Boes: 396

Michael De Rop: 342-4

Robert Dewilde: 8, 10, 13, 17, 20, 24, 26, 28, 30-39, 42-69, 70 (top left and bottom), 71, 74-77, 80-82, 84-90, 93, 95-101, 102 (top right and bottom left and right), 103, 104 (bottom left and right), 105-7, 108 (top), 110-11, 116 (top), 119-23, 132-33, 184-85, 206-7, 236-40, 242-45, 280, 282, 286-89, 298-303, 308-23, 326-32, 334-36, 345-47, 353, 358-59, 370-73, 386, 391-92, 397, 403

Moudi Diab: 333, 338-41

Delphine Gilson: 337

Ferdinand Graf Lückner: 400

Gensho Haga: 2, 4-5, 124-25, 128-31, 168-75, 202-3, 208-9, 211, 216-21, 226-35, 246-55, 350, 355-57, 360-69, 376-85

Gensho Haga and Kiyokazu Nakajima: 212-15, 222-24

Jan Hoogsteyns: 294-95

Kenji Kusakabe: 79, 109

Laurent-Perrier: 348

Steve Lin: 374 (top right)

Marshall Field's: 142

Masaki Miyano: 102 (top left), 176-83, 258-79

Masaki Miyano and Akisuke Shibata: 92, 186-200

Kiyakazu Nakajima: 23, 70 (top right), 72, 78, 83, 104 (top), 108 (bottom), 112-15, 116 (bottom), 117-18, 126-27, 134-41, 210, 225, 290-93, 296-97, 304-7, 354, 374 (all but top right), 375, 395

Kiyakazu Nakajima and Masaki Miyano: 14, 18, 29, 40-41, 73, 144-67, 201, 204-5

Phoenix Seagaia Resort: 256-57

David Lau Reed: 324-25

Guy Sakchai: 285

Wim Van Eesbeek: 241

Phaidon Press Limited
Regent's Wharf
All Saints Street
London N1 9PA

Phaidon Press Inc.
65 Bleecker Street
New York, NY 10012

www.phaidon.com

First published in English 2015
© 2015 Phaidon Press Limited

ISBN 978 0 7148 7052 6

Original edition © 2015 Marot S.A., Brussels
and Daniel Ost, Sint-Niklaas, Belgium

Photographs © 2015 Daniel Ost, Sint-Niklaas, Belgium

"Natural Mystery" © Cees Nooteboom and
"The Art of Integration" © Kengo Kuma

Dutch translation by Patrick Lennon, excluding
Cees Nooteboom's essay "Natural Mystery" translated
by David McKay for Patek Philippe, *Inspirations,* n° 9.
Kengo Kuma's essay "The Art of Integration" translated
from Japanese by Allison Markin Powell.

A CIP catalog record for this book is available from
the Library of Congress and the British Library.

Editorial director, Marot: Jan Martens
Project editor, Marot: Laurent Germeau
Project editor, Phaidon: Sara Bader
Picture researcher: Yann Callaert
Cover design and design concept: YES
Layouts: Juliette de Patoul
Lithography: Mathildestudios

Printed in Belgium

Previous page: Clematis flowers in a glass vase
manifest a kind of pure beauty.

Jacket images:
(front) Berries of *Smilax china*, Ninna-ji,
Kyoto, Japan, 2004.
(back) Folded leaves create a shrine
for a rare Japanese orchid, Kinkaku-ji,
Kyoto, Japan, 2009.